Romeo and

A Tragedy by William Shakespeare

Editor: Patrick Brennan

FOLENS

Editor
Deirdre O'Neill

Design
Karen Hoey

Layout
Oisín Burke

ISBN 978-1-84741-233-1

1623

Contents

Preface

It is not the purpose of the notes that accompany this edition of *Romeo and Juliet* to dispense with either the need to read and study the text or the need for the teacher's guidance in that reading and study. It is hoped that the explanatory notes and the notes following each scene will facilitate both the student's private study of the text itself and also discussion in class under the teacher's guidance. The aim of all study of the play must be that the student familiarises himself or herself with the play and achieves his or her own individual view of it. Thus, nothing stated in these notes should be regarded dogmatically as the only valid view of a topic. **Whatever** is suggested in the notes should be regarded merely **as a guideline or pointer** to stimulate the student's own understanding of the play.

The Explanatory Notes are designed to help towards an understanding of the more difficult words or phrases.

The Notes on each scene include:

(a) A *summary* to help the student to understand what happens in each scene.

(b) A *Scene Analysis* to suggest the significance of each scene in building up the play as a whole.

(c) *Character Analyses* to help the student to get to know the people in the drama as he/she meets them.

The notes at the end of the text need some teacher guidance as they are of a general nature. It is hoped that these pointers towards an overall view of the play will stimulate discussion and thought on the overall significance of *Romeo and Juliet* as a drama.

Finally, the section containing questions should prove useful in the context of the Junior Certificate examination.

This section includes:

(a) Questions on each scene.

(b) General questions.

(c) Past Examination questions, which cover important aspects of the play.

Part 1

INTRODUCTION

Shakespeare's Life and Work

Our knowledge of Shakespeare's life is vague and sketchy. However, there are some details of his life which are clear to us. William Shakespeare was baptised on 26 April 1564 in Holy Trinity Church, Stratford-upon-Avon. He was the third child of John Shakespeare, a tanner and glover, and Mary Arden, who were reasonably wealthy and owned property in Stratford. In 1582 William Shakespeare and Anne Hathway married. They had three children, Susanna, Hamnet and Judith. Later, Shakespeare went to London and made his name, first as an actor and then as a writer of dramas. He became a founder and director of the new Globe Theatre in 1598 and seems to have become quite wealthy. He returned to Stratford and bought the largest house in the town, which further enhanced his status in society. He died on 23 April 1616 and was buried on 25 April, having written at least thirty-seven plays and many poems.

Shakespeare's dramatic writings consist of comedies, histories and tragedies. *Romeo and Juliet* is Shakespeare's earliest tragedy and was written around 1595. His "great" tragedies were written later from 1601 to 1607 and include *Hamlet*, *Othello*, *King Lear* and *Macbeth*, which are probably the most famous of all his writings. Shakespeare also wrote over 150 sonnets on such themes as love, friendship, art and poetry and the ravages of time. Shakespeare was a prolific writer, but his works have stood the test of time and have long been regarded as masterpieces not just for their dramatic skill but especially for their ability to portray a vast range of human emotions.

The Plot Structure

Act 1
The Exposition or Introduction (Act 1, Scenes I to IV).
We learn about the feud in Verona and Romeo's love – melancholy.

Act 2
The Complication (Act 1, Scene V to Act 2, Scene VI)
Romeo and Juliet meet, fall in love and are married secretly.

Act 3
The Climax (Act 3, Scene I)
Tybalt is killed by Romeo to avenge Mercutio's death and Romeo is banished.

Act 4

The Resolution (Act 3, Scene II to Act 5, Scene II)

Romeo and Juliet try to cope with Romeo's banishment and Friar Laurence's plan is put into action to save Juliet from having to marry Paris.

Act 5

The Catastrophe (Act 5, Scene III)

The lovers die tragically and the feuding families are reconciled.

Romeo and Juliet

"Age cannot wither nor custom stale (its) infinite variety," can be applied just as much to Shakespeare's *Romeo and Juliet* as to Cleopatra in *Antony and Cleopatra.* Truly, human life, in all its variety, is to be found in *Romeo and Juliet.* Its twenty-four scenes contain within them tragedy for the thoughtful, comedy for the light-hearted, depth of feeling for the sympathetic, idealism and passion for the romantic, morality for the serious-minded and inspiration and hope for the pessimistic, as well as some fine poetry for the literary-minded. Few dramas, whether Shakespearean or modern, can boast such universal appeal and it is little wonder that almost a dozen different operas – to say nothing of films and stage-shows – have been composed with *Romeo and Juliet* as their basis. *West Side Story,* for example, portrays a more modern *Romeo and Juliet* amid the slums and gang-warfare of New York. Little surprise then that *Romeo and Juliet* has become a firm favourite with all ages and tastes.

Romeo and Juliet was written by William Shakespeare, probably in 1595, and it was his first tragedy. The story was familiar to the people of Shakespeare's day and appeared in a collection of stories called *Novelle* by Matheo Bandello, published in 1554 and later translated into French by Pierre Borstean. Arthur Brooke based his long poem, *The Tragicall Hystory of Romeo and Juliet,* on the French version, and it was this poem of Brooke's that was the main source of Shakespeare's play, *Romeo and Juliet.* Shakespeare adapted his sources to suit his own purposes, enlivening the characters and intensifying the emotions in the play, and the resulting masterpiece far surpasses its sources.

Finally, Shakespeare's *Romeo and Juliet* has much to say to the modern world on varied topics of remarkable relevance to this age: peace and war; love and hate; consideration and misunderstanding; hope and fear; fidelity in love; courage and self-sacrifice and, above all, the unnecessary waste of human resources in a world which needs to slow down and take stock of itself before it is too late.

Romeo and Juliet has much to say to the younger generation too, concerning such momentous matters as youthful infatuation, falling madly in love, parental misunderstandings, desperate remedies to overcome the restrictive demands of society, self-reliance and personal integrity, despite the pressures to conform, and how the young can teach the older members of society about peace and reconciliation. Everyone can find something to attract and inspire him or her in *Romeo and Juliet* and that is the index of Shakespeare's unsurpassed achievement in the art of portraying real human situations and feelings.

Characters

Escalus	Prince of Verona
Paris	a young Nobleman, Kinsman of the Prince
Montague } Capulet }	Heads of two Houses at variance with each other
Uncle to Capulet	
Romeo	Son to Montague
Mercutio Benvolio	Kinsman to the Prince } Nephew to Montague } Friends to Romeo
Tybalt	Nephew to Lady Capulet
Friar Laurence	a Franciscan
Friar John	of the same Order
Balthasar	Servant to Romeo
Sampson } Gregory }	Servants to Capulet
Peter	Servant to Juliet's Nurse
Abraham	Servant to Montague
An Apothecary	
Three Musicians	
Page to Mercutio; Page to Paris; another Page; an Officer	
Lady Montague	Wife to Montague
Lady Capulet	Wife to Capulet
Juliet	Daughter to Capulet
Nurse to Juliet	
Citizens of Verona; male and female Kinsfolk to both Houses; Masquers, Guards, Watchmen and Attendants	
Chorus	
Scene	Verona: Once (in the Fifth Act), at Mantua.

Part 2
Text and Commentary

Prologue

The Capulets and Montague were both equal
   Scene was set in Verona, Italy,
   An old grudge breaks & into
new violence,
   where blood of the incent citizens
   make bloody hands unclean
The children of these enemys fall
in love with each other who take
tak there own lifes.
Whose missfortunate set-back
But only the death of them would stop
the feud.
The fearful passage of their death sparked love,
   And the long standing family feuds
with only their childrens death, stop it

Act 1

Prologue

Enter Chorus

Chorus.

Two households, both alike in dignity[1]
  In fair Verona, where we lay our scene,
From ancient grudge break to new mutiny,[2]
  Where civil blood makes civil hands unclean.[3]
From forth the fatal loins of these two foes
  A pair of star-cross'd[4] lovers take their life;
Whose misadventur'd[5] piteous overthrows[6]
  Doth with their death bury their parents' strife.
The fearful passage of their death-mark'd love,
  And the continuance of their parents' rage,   *10*
Which, but their children's end, nought could
     remove,
  Is now the two hours' traffick[7] of our stage;
The which if you with patient ears attend,
What here shall miss, our toil[8] shall strive to mend

                                [Exit

[1] rank

[2] violence

[3] bloodshed corrupts the citizens

[4] ill-fated, unlucky

[5] misfortunate

[6] set-backs

[7] duration

[8] our efforts will make up for whatever is lacking

Summary

A Tragedy of Love in the Midst of Hate

A Chorus, usually a single announcer, calls the audience to attention by introducing them to the topics of the play in a formal sonnet.

– The first four lines bring us to Verona, in northern Italy, the scene of the play. Verona is disturbed by the long-standing feud which has broken out yet again between two noble families, the Montagues and the Capulets.

– The second quatrain foretells the healing of this rift in society through the deaths of two ill-fated children of these families who tragically force their parents to see sense and make peace.

– The third quatrain tells the audience that the drama about the ill-fated lovers and their feuding parents will last two hours.

– The final two lines appeal to the audience to watch patiently as the actors do their best to entertain them with this tragic story.

Scene Analysis

(i) Tragic Themes

The Prologue emphasises that the main themes of the drama will be the tragic "*star-cross'd*" love of Romeo and Juliet and the social strife between the noble families of Verona. The romance of the lovers is placed firmly in the social context of hatred and feuding. The play is to be tragic in nature and the Prologue prepares the audience for the worst that will happen.

(ii) Information

The Prologue provides the audience with sufficient information to arouse their curiosity regarding what is about to happen in their presence. The audience now knows in outline what will happen – that two children of the rival families will fall in love and, by their deaths, will restore peace and harmony between their families but alas too late. Naturally the audience is curious to know how this will come about and will be all the more attentive as the drama unfolds.

Characters

The Chorus in classical drama was a group of characters whose role it was to comment on and interpret the action of the play. The Chorus here is a single, formal announcer who directs the audience towards a tragic view of the ensuing events.

Scene 1

Verona. A Public Place

Enter Sampson and Gregory, armed with swords and bucklers.

Sampson
Gregory, on my word, we'll not carry coals.[1]

Gregory
No, for then we should be colliers.[2]

Sampson
I mean, an we be in choler,[3] we'll draw.

Gregory
Ay, while you live, draw your neck out o' the collar.

Sampson
I strike quickly, being moved.

Gregory
But thou art not quickly moved to strike.

[1] put up with insults

[2] coal-miners or sellers

[3] anger

Sampson
A dog of the house of Montague moves me.

Gregory
To move is to stir, and to be valiant is to stand;
therefore, if thou art moved, thou runnest away.

Sampson
A dog of that house shall move me to stand: I will   *10*
take the wall of any man or maid of Montague's.

Gregory
That shows thee a weak slave; for the weakest
goes to the wall.[4]

[4]loses out, is pushed back

Sampson
'Tis true; and therefore women, being the weaker
vessels, are ever thrust to the wall: therefore I will
push Montague's men from the wall, and thrust his
maids to the wall.

Gregory
The quarrel is between our masters and us their men.

Sampson
'Tis all one, I will show myself a tyrant: when I
have fought with the men, I will be cruel with the   *20*
maids; I will cut off their heads.

Gregory
Draw thy tool; here comes two of the house of the
        Montagues.

Enter Abraham and Balthasar

Sampson
My naked weapon is out; quarrel, I will back thee.

Gregory
How! turn thy back and run?

Sampson
Fear me not.

Gregory
No, marry; I fear thee!

Sampson
Let us take the law of our sides;[5] let them begin.

[5]keep on the right side of
the law

Gregory
I will frown as I pass by, and let them take it
as they list.

Sampson
Nay, as they dare. I will bite my thumb at them; — insult   30
which is a disgrace to them, if they bear it.

Abraham
Do you bite your thumb at us, sir?

Sampson [*Aside to Gregory*]
Is the law of our side if I say ay?

Gregory [*Aside to Sampson*]
No.

Sampson
No, sir, I do not bite my thumb at you, sir; but I bite
my thumb, sir.

Gregory
Do you quarrel, sir?

Abraham
Quarrel, sir! no, sir.

Sampson
If you do, sir, I am for you: I serve as good a man
as you.   40

Abraham
No better.

Sampson
Well, sir.

Gregory [*Aside to Sampson*]
Say, 'better'; here comes one of my master's kinsmen.

Sampson
Yes, better, sir.

Abraham
You lie.

Sampson
Draw, if you be men. Gregory, remember thy
⁶slashing   swashing⁶ blow.

[*They fight*

Enter Benvolio

Benvolio
Part, fools!
Put up your swords; you know not what you do.

[*Beats down their swords*

Enter Tybalt

Tybalt
What! art thou drawn among these heartless   50
    hinds?[7]   [7]cowardly peasants
Turn thee, Benvolio, look upon thy death.

Benvolio
I do but keep the peace: put up thy sword,
Or manage it to part these men with me.

Tybalt
What! drawn, and talk of peace? I hate the word,
As I hate hell, all Montagues, and thee. _Fieshtyspeshire_
Have at thee, coward!   [They fight

*Enter several persons of both houses, who join the fray; then
        enter Citizens, with clubs and partisans.*

Citizens
Clubs, bills, and partisans![8] strike! beat them   [8]kinds of pike
down!
Down with the Capulets! down with the
Montagues!   60

Enter Capulet in his gown and Lady Capulet

Capulet
What noise is this? Give me my long sword, ho!

Lady Capulet
A crutch, a crutch! Why call you for a sword?

Capulet
My sword, I say! Old Montague is come,
And flourishes his blade in spite of me.

Enter Montague and Lady Montague

Montague
Thou villain Capulet! Hold me not; let me go.

Lady Montague
Thou shalt not stir one foot to seek a foe.

Enter Prince with his Train

Prince
Rebellious subjects, enemies to peace,
Profaners of this neighbour-stained steel, —
Will they not hear? What ho! you men, you beasts,
That quench the fire of your pernicious rage   70

⁹badly made weapons or
weapons used angrily

¹⁰dignified

¹¹rusted with disuse

¹²open

¹³thereby

¹⁴on different sides

With purple fountains issuing from your veins,
On pain of torture, from those bloody hands
Throw your mis-temper'd⁹ weapons to the ground,
And hear the sentence of your moved prince.
Three civil brawls, bred of an airy word,
By thee, old Capulet, and Montague,
Have thrice disturb'd the quiet of our streets,
And made Verona's ancient citizens
Cast by their grave beseeming¹⁰ ornaments,
To wield old partisans, in hands as old,   80
Canker'd with peace,¹¹ to part your canker'd hate.
If ever you disturb our streets again
Your lives shall pay the forfeit of the peace. _NB warning to both family_
For this time, all the rest depart away:
You, Capulet, shall go along with me;
And, Montague, come you this afternoon
To know our further pleasure in this case,
To old Free-town, our common judgment-place.
Once more, on pain of death, all men depart.
          [Exeunt all but Montague, Lady Montague, and Benvolio

Montague
Who set this ancient quarrel new abroach?¹²   90
Speak, nephew, were you by when it began?
Benvolio _Gives a truthful unbised acount_
Here were the servants of your adversary
And yours close fighting ere I did approach:
I drew to part them; in the instant came
The fiery Tybalt, with his sword prepar'd,
Which, as he breath'd defiance to my ears,
He swung about his head, and cut the winds,
Who, nothing hurt withal¹³ hiss'd him in scorn.
While we were interchanging thrusts and blows,
Came more and more, and fought on part and
          part,¹⁴   100
Till the prince came, who parted either part.

Lady Montague
O! where is Romeo? saw you him to-day?
Right glad I am he was not at this fray.

Benvolio
Madam, an hour before the worshipp'd sun
Peer'd forth the golden window of the east,
A troubled mind drave me to walk abroad;
Where, underneath the grove of sycamore

That westward rooteth from the city's side,
So early walking did I see your son:
Towards him I made; but he was ware[15] of me,   *110*   [15]aware
And stole into the covert of the wood:
I, measuring his affections by my own,
That most are busied when they're most alone,
Pursu'd my humour[16] not pursuing his,   [16]inclination
And gladly shunn'd who gladly fled from me.

Montague

Many a morning hath he there been seen,
With tears augmenting the fresh morning's dew,
Adding to clouds more clouds with his deep sighs;
But all so soon as the all-cheering sun
Should in the furthest east begin to draw   *120*
The shady curtains from Aurora's bed,[17]   [17]dawn
Away from light steals home my heavy[18] son,   [18]sad
And private in his chamber pens[19] himself,   [19]locks
Shuts up his windows, locks fair daylight out,
And makes himself an artificial night.
Black and portentous must this humour[20] prove *we learn that romeo is*   [20]mood
Unless good counsel may the cause remove.

Benvolio

My noble uncle, do you know the cause?

Montague

I neither know it nor can learn of him.

Benvolio

Have you importun'd[21] him by any means?   *130*   [21]questioned

Montague

Both by myself and many other friends:
But he, his own affections' counsellor,
Is to himself, I will not say how true,
But to himself so secret and so close,
So far from sounding[22] and discovery,   [22]measuring
As is the bud bit with an envious worm,
Ere he can spread his sweet leaves to the air,
Or dedicate his beauty to the sun.
Could we but learn from whence his sorrows grow,
We would as willingly give cure as know.   *140*

Benvolio

See where he comes: so please you, step aside;
I'll know his grievance, or be much denied.

Montague

I would thou wert so happy by thy stay,

To hear true shriff.[23] Come, madam, let's away.

[Exeunt Montague and Lady

Enter Romeo

Benvolio

Good morrow, cousin.

Romeo

                              Is the day so young?

Benvolio

But new struck nine.

Romeo

                                        Ay me! sad hours seem long.

Was that my father that went hence so fast?

Benvolio

It was. What sadness lengthens Romeo's hours?

Romeo

Not having that, which having, makes them short.

Benvolio

In love?   *150*

Romeo

Out —

Benvolio

Of love?

Romeo

Out of her favour, where I am in love.

Benvolio

Alas! that love, so gentle in his view,

Should be so tyrannous and rough in proof.

Romeo

Alas! that love, whose view is muffled[24] still,

Should, without eyes, see pathways to his will.

Where shall we dine? O me! What fray was here?

Yet tell me not, for I have heard it all.

Here's much to do with hate, but more with love: *160*

Why then, O brawling love! O loving hate!

O any thing! of nothing first create.

O heavy lightness! serious vanity!

Mis-shapen chaos of well-seeming forms![25]

Feather of lead, bright smoke, cold fire, sick health!

Still-waking sleep,[26] that is not what it is!

[23]true confession

[24]blindfolded

unrequited love

[25]things that look beautiful

[26]sleeplessness

This love feel I, that feel no love in this.
Dost thou not laugh?

Benvolio
                              No, coz,[27] I rather weep.   [27]cousin

Romeo
Good heart, at what?

Benvolio
At thy good heart's oppression.   *170*

Romeo
Why, such is love's transgression.[28]   [28]fault, disadvantage
Griefs of mine own lie heavy in my breast,
Which thou wilt propagate[29] to have it press'd   [29]increase
With more of thine: this love that thou hast shown
Doth add more grief to too much of mine own.
Love is a smoke made with the fume of sighs;
Being purg'd,[30] a fire sparkling in lovers' eyes;   [30]purified
Being vex'd,[31] a sea nourish'd with lovers' tears: [31]angered
What is it else? a madness most discreet,[32]   [32]discriminating
A choking gall, and a preserving sweet.   *180*
Farewell, my coz.

Benvolio   *[Going.*
                       Soft,[33] I will go along;   [33]hold on
And if you leave me so, you do me wrong.

Romeo
Tut! I have lost myself; I am not here;
This is not Romeo, he's some other where.

Benvolio
Tell me in sadness,[34] who is that you love?   [34]seriously

Romeo
What! shall I groan and tell thee?

Benvolio
                        Groan! why, no;
But sadly tell me who.

Romeo
Bid a sick man in sadness make his will;
Ah! word ill urg'd to one that is so ill.
In sadness, cousin, I do love a woman.   *190*

Benvolio
I aim'd so near when I suppos'd you lov'd.

Romeo
A right good mark-man! And she's fair I love.

Benvolio

A right fair mark, fair coz, is soonest hit.

Romeo

Well, in that hit you miss: she'll not be hit

With Cupid's³⁵ arrow; she hath Dian's³⁶ wit;

And, in strong proof of chasity well arm'd,

From love's weak childish bow she lives

      uncharm'd.

She will not stay the siege of loving terms,³⁷

Nor bide³⁸ the encounter of assailing eyes,

Nor ope her lap to saint-seducing gold: 200

O! she is rich in beauty; only poor

That, when she dies, with beauty dies her store.³⁹

Benvolio

Then she hath sworn that she will still live chaste?

Romeo

She hath, and in that sparing makes huge waste;

For beauty, starv'd with her severity,

Cuts beauty off from all posterity.

She is too fair, too wise, wisely too fair,

To merit bliss by making me despair:

She hath forsworn to love, and in that vow

Do I live dead that live to tell it now.   210

Benvolio

Be rul'd by me; forget to think of her.

Romeo

O! teach me how I should forget to think.

Benvolio

By giving liberty unto thine eyes:

Examine other beauties.

Romeo

              'Tis the way,

To call hers exquisite, in question more.

These happy masks that kiss fair laidies' brows

Being black put us in mind they hide the fair;

He, that is strucken blind cannot forget

The precious treasure of his eyesight lost:

Show me a mistress that is passing fair,   220

What doth her beauty serve but as a note

Where I may read who pass'd that passing fair?

Farewell: thou canst not teach me to forget.

Benvolio

I'll pay that doctrine,⁴⁰ or else die in debt.   *[Exeunt*

³⁵God of love
³⁶Diana, goddess of chastity

³⁷words of love
³⁸put up with

³⁹children

⁴⁰teach you (to forget)

12

If ever you disturb our streets again
Your lives shall pay the forfeit of the peace.

(Prince, Act 1, Scene I)

Summary – Time: 9 a.m. on Sunday morning

THE SETTING OF THE DRAMA

The Street Battle

The scene opens with the Capulet servants, Sampson and Gregory, complaining about a recent skirmish with the Montague servants. They boast to each other about their bravery and their sexual abilities.

Then the Montague servants, Abraham and Balthasar, arrive. Sampson provokes a quarrel by biting his thumb at the Montagues. Both sides hesitate to fight. The sight of Tybalt, a nephew of the Capulets, leads Gregory to taunt Sampson, resulting in a fight with Abraham.

Benvolio arrives and attemps to break up the fight, but Tybalt misunderstands Benvolio's action and attacks him. Others join in and a street battle follows. Montague and Capulet try to intervene but are restrained by their wives.

In the midst of the brawl, Escalus, Prince of Verona, enters and, with difficulty, quells the riot. He accuses Montague and Capulet of stirring up unrest and disturbing the peace of the citizens of Verona and promises death to anyone who disturbs the peace again. Then he leaves with Capulet and the stage is cleared.

Romeo Introduced

As Benvolio explains to Montague how the fight began, Lady Montague begins to wonder where her son Romeo was during the riot. We then learn of Romeo's solitary wanderings and moods which his father cannot understand. As Romeo enters, Benvolio decides to find out what is amiss with Romeo. Romeo declares he is sad because the lady he loves does not care for him: Romeo is in love with the beauty of a lady who wishes to be chaste. Benvolio advises Romeo to forget her and seek out other beauties, but Romeo says these will only remind him of the most beautiful lady of all whom he loves. Benvolio resolves to make Romeo forget.

Scene Analysis

The Social Scene and Its Background

The world of Verona is not a place of peace and humour as might seem the case from the comic exchanges of the Capulet servants. It is a world of civil strife in which all are involved, from servants to masters.

Prince Escalus makes clear that this rioting we witness is not the first: there have been *"three civil brawls"* in the recent past which have disturbed the peace of Verona's streets. It is so serious that the Prince threatens death to those who disturb the peace from now on:

> *"If ever you disturb our streets again*
> *Your lives shall pay the forfeit of the peace."*

Everyone is tired of the riots and violence. Yet all will join in with the slightest provocation. Violence has taken control. Such an atmosphere is likely to provoke tragic consequences.

Romeo in Love

The love of Romeo for his unattainable lady is in marked contrast to the hatred and disharmony on Verona's streets. Only Romeo is ready for love in a world of hate. Is Romeo to be the deliverer of this strife-ridden society so much in need of the healing of real love?

Yet Romeo's love is as painful as the violence in society. He causes pain and worry to his parents and to himself by his continual wanderings and by his depressed state of mind. Romeo too is in need of deliverance from the burden of his unreturned love of Rosaline, whom he is unwilling to name in this scene.

Characters

THE CAPULETS

The Capulets seem to be more fiery in character than the Montagues.

Tybalt is hot-headed and easily provoked to anger. His presence in this scene stirs up the brawl between the rival servants. He says to Benvolio:

> *"What! drawn, and talk of peace? I hate the word,*
> *As I hate hell, all Montagues, and thee.*
> *Have at thee, coward!"*

Old Capulet is eager for violence and calls for a sword to rush into the confrontation when a crutch might have been more appropriate.

Lady Capulet acts as a peacemaker in this scene.

THE MONTAGUES

The Montagues are more eager for peace than the Capulets.

Old Montague is more concerned that strife has again arisen than with fighting his enemies.

Lady Montague is more anxious for the safety of Romeo than for the result of the riot.

> *"O where is Romeo?"*

Benvolio, the nephew of Montague, plays an important role in this scene. He is the peace-maker who tries to avert another brawl.

> *"Put up your swords; you know not what you do."*

he says to the fighting servants.

He is not a coward, but truly desires peace.

> *"I do but keep the peace:"*

He shows common sense in his advice to Romeo to *"forget to think"* of Rosaline. He is a loyal friend to Romeo when he needs him most.

> *"I'll pay that doctrine, or else die in debt."*

ROMEO

Romeo is the typical adolescent lover who is melancholy in nature, moody and romantic.

> *"Many a morning hath he there been seen,*
> *With tears augmenting the fresh morning's dew,*
> *Adding to clouds more clouds with his deep sighs;"*

He is more *"in love with love"* than with Rosaline, whom he is unwilling to name. Love for Romeo is:

> *"a smoke made with the fume of sighs;"*
> *"a fire sparkling in lovers' eyes;"*
> *"a sea nourish'd with lovers' tears:"*
> *"a madness... A choking gall... a preserving sweet."*

Yet we are made aware of another side of Romeo. *"This is not Romeo,"* Romeo tells Benvolio. His anti-social behaviour and depression have a real cause in that Rosaline has sworn to live *"chaste"* (unmarried). Romeo regrets that *"in that sparing [she] makes huge waste"* since she *"with her severity, Cuts beauty off from all posterity"*. One wonders is Romeo depressed because he cannot marry Rosaline or is his love simply an infatuation with an unattainable ideal of love. Certainly Romeo is seen as going through a bad phase of wounded self-esteem which prevents him from seeing clearly what he ought to do.

THE SERVANTS

The servants are all comic characters who show the cruder side of love in their jesting. Sampson boasts much of his ability as a lover. He is afraid to start a quarrel with the Montagues without Gregory's support. Gregory shows more shrewdness and it is he who contrives the fight by using Sampson as a tool to insult the Montagues. The Montague servants are not really characters but types who, by their stupidity, allow themselves to be drawn into a quarrel by Sampson and Gregory.

Scene II

The Same. A Street. Enter Capulet, Paris, and Servant

Capulet

But Montague is bound[1] as well as I,

In penalty alike; and 'tis not hard, I think,

For men so old as we to keep the peace.

Paris

Of honourable reckoning[2] are you both;

And pity 'tis you liv'd at odds[3] so long.

But now, my lord, what say you to my suit? ~ *Seeking meaning*

Capulet

But saying o'er what I have said before: ~ *Too young to marry*

My child is yet a stranger in the world,

She hath not seen the change of fourteen years;

Let two more summers wither in their pride   10

Ere we may think her ripe to be a bride.

Paris

Younger than she are happy mothers made.

Capulet

And too soon marr'd are those so early made.

Earth hath swallow'd all my hopes[4] but she,

She is the hopeful lady of my earth:

But woo her, gentle Paris, get her heart,

My will to her consent is but a part;

An[5] she agree, within her scope of choice[6]

Lies my consent and fair according voice.[7]

This night I hold an old accustom'd feast,   20

Whereto I have invited many a guest

Such as I love; and you, among the store,

One more, most welcome, makes my number

     more.

At my poor house look to behold this night

Earth-treading stars[8] that make dark heaven light:

Such comfort as do lusty young men feel

When well-apparel'd April on the heel

Of limping winter treads, even such delight

Among fresh female buds shall you this night

Inherit[9] at my house; hear all, all see,   30

And like her most whose merit most shall be:

Which on more view of, many, mine being one,

May stand in number,[10] though in reckoning[11]

    none.

[1] obliged under threat of death

[2] reputation

[3] have been enemies

[4] children

[5] if

[6] according to her wishes

[7] agreement

[8] beautiful women

[9] see

[10] be among

[11] beauty

Come, go with me.

                    [To Servant, giving him a paper] Go,

            sirrah, trudge about
Through fair Verona; find those persons out
Whose names are written there, and to them say,
My house and welcome on their pleasure stay.¹²

                    [Exeunt Capulet and Paris

Servant
Find them out whose names are written here! It is
written that the shoemaker should meddle with his
yard, and the tailor with his last, the fisher with his   *40*
pencil, and the painter with his nets; but I am sent
to find those persons, whose names are here writ,
and can never find what names the writing person
hath here writ. I must to the learned. In good time.

                  [enter Benvolio and Romeo

Benvolio
Tut! man, one fire burns out another's burning,
One pain is lessen'd by another's anguish;
Turn giddy, and be holp¹³ by backward turning;
One desperate grief cures with another's languish:
Take thou some new infection¹⁴ to thy eye,
And the rank poison of the old will die.   *50*

Romeo
Your plantain leaf is excellent for that.

Benvolio
For what, I pray thee?

Romeo

                  For your broken shin.

Benvolio
Why, Romeo, art thou mad?

Romeo
Not mad, but bound more than a madman is;
Shut up in prison, kept without my food,
Whipp'd and tormented, and — Good den,¹⁵
      good fellow.

Servant
God gi' good den. I pray, sir, can you read?

Romeo
Ay, mine own fortune in my misery.

¹²await

¹³be helped

¹⁴interest

¹⁵Good evening

Servant
Perhaps you have learn'd it without book: but,
I pray, can you read any thing you see?   *60*

Romeo
Ay, if I know the letters and the language.

Servant
Ye say honestly; rest you merry!   *[Offering to go*

Romeo
Stay, fellow; I can read.
Signior Martino and his wife and daughters; County
Anselme and his beauteous sisters; the lady widow
of Vitruvio; Signior Placentio, and his lovely nieces;
Mercutio and his brother Valentine; mine uncle
Capulet, his wife and daughters; my fair niece
Rosaline; Livia; Signior Valentio and his cousin
Tybalt; Lucio and the lively Helena.   *70*
A fair assembly: whither should they come?

Servant
Up.

Romeo
Whither?

Servant
To supper; to our house.

Romeo
Whose house?

Servant
My master's.

Romeo
Indeed, I should have asked you that before.

Servant
Now I'll tell you without asking. My master is the
great rich Capulet; and if you be not of the house
of Montagues, I pray, come and crush a cup of   *80*
wine. Rest you merry!
                                                    [Exit

Benvolio
At this same ancient feast of Capulet's,   *refers to romeo love*
Sups the fair Rosaline, whom thou so lov'st,
With all the admired beauties of Verona:
Go thither; and, with unattainted[16] eye   [16]impartial, unbiased
Compare her face with some that I shall show,
And I will make thee think thy swan a crow.

Romeo
When the devout religion of mine eye
Maintains such falsehood, then turns tears to fires!
And these, who often drown'd could never die,   *90*
Transparent[17] heretics, be burnt for liars!
One fairer than my love! the all-seeing sun
Ne'er saw her match since first the world begun.

Benvolio
Tut! you saw her fair, none else being by,
Herself pois'd with herself in either eye;
But in that crystal scales[18] let there be weigh'd
Your lady's love against some other maid
That I will show you shining at this feast,
And she shall scant[19] show well that now shows
    best.

Romeo
I'll go along, no such sight to be shown,   *100*
But to rejoice in a splendour of mine own.[20]

                  [Exeunt

[17]obvious

[18]Romeo's eyes

[19]hardly, scarcely

[20]Rosaline

Summary – Time: Sunday afternoon

PARIS AND ROMEO

Capulet Interviews Paris

Paris, who is Prince Escalus' cousin, is returning with Capulet from the Prince's judgement on the recent riot. Paris seeks Capulet's consent to his marrying Juliet. Capulet refuses since Juliet is barely fourteen years old and is his only child and heir. He also wishes Juliet to show her own choice of suitor. Paris is invited to judge Juliet among the fair women of Verona at a feast that night in Capulet's house. A guest list is handed to a servant who is to inform the guests of the feast. The servant is not able to read.

The Guests at Capulet's Feast

The servant seeks the help of Benvolio and Romeo who are discussing Romeo's depression. Benvolio advises Romeo to get some new infection of love to rid him of his love of Rosaline. Then Romeo reads the guest list for the servant, thus finding an opportunity to see that Rosaline is invited to the feast. Benvolio hopes to show Romeo that other women surpass Rosaline's beauty in order to make Romeo more realistic in his attitude.

Scene Analysis

Paris Goes

Hopes are aroused that there will be an end to the feuding between the rival families.

Capulet and Paris both desire peace. Paris says:

> "And pity 'tis you liv'd at odds so long."

Romeo's Opportunity

Ironically this scene also provides Romeo with an opportunity to go to Capulet's feast where he hopes to see Rosaline (but will meet Juliet).

It becomes clear how unrealistic and extravagant Romeo's love for Rosaline really is. He says:

> "One fairer than my love! the all-seeing sun
> Ne'er saw her match since first the world begun."

Yet his love is deep and Benvolio's remedy of *"some new infection to thy eye"* looks forward to the *"love at first sight"* of Romeo for Juliet in *Act 1 Scene V*. This scene suggests that Romeo may solve his love problem but not in the way either he or Benvolio thinks.

Characters

OLD CAPULET

He is a loving father concerned with his daughter's happiness in life through marriage:

> "She is the hopeful lady of my earth:"

He is considerate of his daughter's own wishes, realising how young she is:

> "...within her scope of choice
> Lies my consent..."

He appeals to Paris to avoid rushing into a marriage with her.

He shows himself to be a generous, hospitable person by inviting Paris to win Juliet's love at the feast for his friends. He wishes for harmony in his world:

> "'tis not hard, I think,
> For men so old as we to keep the peace."

PARIS

He is a nobleman of good family, a cousin of Prince Escalus.

He desires peace in Verona:

> "And pity 'tis you lived at odds so long."

He is determined to win Juliet in marriage:

> "Younger than she are happy mothers made."

His motives are unclear, but there is no evidence that he loves Juliet.

ROMEO

Romeo is capable of deep, passionate love. He sees love as a religion which binds him to it. Romeo believes in the power of his love to withstand the test proposed by Benvolio, of comparison with others. Romeo is sincere in his love.

Yet Romeo's love is too extravagant to be true

> *"I'll go along, no such sight to be shown,*
> *But to rejoice in a splendour of mine own."*

He is the typical lover of the love poets who adores his love at a distance as the most beautiful of all women.

Scene III

The Same. A Room in Capulet's House
Enter Lady Capulet and Nurse

Lady Capulet
Nurse, where's my daughter? call her forth to me.

Nurse
Now, by my maidenhead, at twelve year old, —
I bade her come. What, lamb! what, ladybird!
God forbid! where's this girl? what, Juliet!

Enter Juliet

Juliet
How now! who calls?

Nurse
                    Your mother.

Juliet
                                        Madam, I am here.
What is your will?

Lady Capulet
This is the matter. Nurse, give leave awhile.[1]
We must talk in secret: nurse, come back again;
I have remember'd me, thou's[2] hear our counsel.
Thou know'st my daughter's of a pretty age.   *10*

Nurse
Faith, I can tell her age unto an hour.

Lady Capulet
She's not fourteen.

[1] leave us for a while

[2] thou shalt

Nurse
> I'll lay fourteen of my teeth —
And yet to my teen[3] be it spoken I have but four —
She is not fourteen. How long is it now
To Lammas-tide?[4]

[3] sorrow

[4] 1 August

Lady Capulet
> A fortnight and odd days.

Nurse
Even or odd, of all days in the year,
Come Lammas-eve at night shall she be fourteen.
Susan and she — God rest all Christian souls! —
Were of an age.[5] Well, Susan is with God;
She was too good for me. But, as I said,   *20*
On Lammas-eve at night shall she be fourteen;
That shall she, marry; I remember it well.
'Tis since the earthquake now eleven years;
And she was wean'd, I never shall forget it,
Of all the days of the year, upon that day;
For I had then laid wormwood[6] to my dug,[7]
Sitting in the sun under the dove-house wall;
My lord and you were then at Mantua.
Nay, I do bear a brain:[8] — but, as I said,
When it did taste the wormwood on the nipple   *30*
Of my dug and felt it bitter, pretty fool!
To see it tetchy[9] and fall out with the dug.
'Shake,' quoth[10] the dove-house: 'twas no need,
      I trow,[11]
To bid me trudge:
And since that time it is eleven years;
For then she could stand high lone; nay, by the
      rood,[12]
She could have run and waddled all about;
For even the day before she broke her brow:
And then my husband — God be with his soul!
A' was a merry man — took up the child: *40*
'Yea,' quoth he, 'dost thou fall upon thy face?
Thou wilt fall backward when thou hast more wit;
Wilt thou not, Jule?' and, by my halidom,
The pretty wretch left crying, and said 'Ay'.
To see now how a jest shall come about!
I warrant, an I should live a thousand years,   *50*
I never should forget it: 'Wilt thou not, Jule?' quoth
      he;
And, pretty fool, it stinted and said 'Ay'.

[5] the same age

[6] a bitter herb
[7] breast

[8] I remember well

[9] irritable
[10] began (to shake)
[11] believe

[12] cross

Lady Capulet

Enough of this; I pray thee, hold thy peace.

Nurse

Yes, madam. Yet I cannot choose but laugh,   50
To think it should leave crying, and say 'Ay'.
And yet, I warrant, it had upon its brow
A bump as big as a young cockerel's stone;
A perilous knock; and it cried bitterly:
'Yea,' quoth my husband, 'fall'st upon thy face
Thou wilt fall backward when thou com'st to age;
Wilt thou not, Jule?' it stinted and said 'Ay'.

Juliet

And stint thou too, I pray thee, nurse, say I.

Nurse

Peace, I have done. God mark thee to his grace!
Thou wast the prettiest babe that e'er I nursed: 60
An I might live to see thee married once,
I have my wish.

Lady Capulet

Marry,[13] that 'marry' is the very theme
I came to talk of. Tell me, daughter Juliet,
How stands your disposition to be married?

Juliet

It is an honour that I dream not of.

Nurse

An honour! were not I thine only nurse,
I would say thou hast suck'd wisdom from thy teat.

Lady Capulet

Well, think of marriage now; younger than you,
Here in Verona, ladies of esteem,   70
Are made already mothers: by my count,
I was your mother much upon these years
That you are now a maid. Thus then in brief,
The valiant Paris seeks you for his love.

Nurse

A man, young lady! lady, such a man
As all the world — why, he's a man of wax.[14]

Lady Capulet

Verona's summer hath not such a flower.

Nurse

Nay, he's a flower; in faith, a very flower.

[13]by Mary

[14]a perfect man

Lady Capulet
What say you? can you love the gentleman?
This night you shall behold him at our feast;   80
Read o'er the volume of young Paris' face
And find delight writ there with beauty's pen;
Examine every married lineament,[15]   [15]harmonious feature
And see how one another lends content;[16]   [16]enhance
And what obscur'd in this fair volume lies
Find written in the margent[17] of his eyes.   [17]margin
This precious book of love, this unbound lover,
To beautify him, only lacks a cover:
The fish lives in the sea, and 'tis much pride
For fair without[18] the fair within[19] to hide: 90   [18]outer beauty
                                                                                        [19]inner beauty
That book in many eyes doth share the glory,
That in gold clasps locks in the golden story:
So shall you share all that he doth possess,
By having him making yourself no less.
Speak briefly, can you like of[20] Paris' love?   [20]accept

Juliet
I'll look to like, if looking liking move;   *Obedient clause*
But no more deep will I endart mine eye
Than your consent gives strength to make it fly.

Dramatic irony –
audience know more
than the characters

Enter a Servant

Servant
Madam, the guests are come, supper served up,
you called, my young lady asked for, the nurse   100
cursed in the pantry, and everything in extremity.
I must hence to wait;[21] I beseech you, follow   [21]to serve
straight.

Lady Capulet
We follow thee. Juliet, the county stays.[22]   [22]the court waits

Nurse
Go, girl, seek happy nights to happy days.   [Exeunt

Summary – Time: Later on Sunday afternoon

Juliet's Future Considered

Lady Capulet wishes to persuade Juliet to consider seriously Paris's proposal of marriage, but the Nurse babbles on and on in a comic manner about how she reared Juliet with great affection and care. Lady Capulet recommends Paris to Juliet as an ideal match for her in the view of society while the nurse reminds Juliet of the physical aspect of marriage. Juliet in reply says she will try her best to like Paris in obedience to her mother. Then a servant interrupts to summon them to the feast which has already begun.

Scene Analysis

Juliet's World

Juliet is confronted with Paris's proposal of marriage by Lady Capulet who emphasises the demand of society that Juliet makes a good marriage. Paris is presented by Lady Capulet as an ideal match for Juliet. Juliet listens dutifully, but is not wholehearted in her agreement:

> *"I'll look to like, if looking liking move;"*

The nurse presents us and Juliet with a contrasting view of marriage to Lady Capulet's social view. The nurse emphasises the physical aspects of love and marriage:

> *"Go, girl, seek happy nights to happy days."*

Juliet herself shows maturity in assessing these proposals. She will observe before she chooses a husband. She is not looking for a social match, like her mother, nor mere physical love, like the nurse:

> *'I'll look to like,"*

Like Romeo in *Scene II*, she is ready for real love when she sees it.

Characters

JULIET

Juliet is young as we know from her father in *Scene II*. She has not yet seriously contemplated marriage:

> *"It is an honour that I dream not of."*

Marriage at fourteen would not be all that unusual in the context of the play.

Juliet is a dutiful and respectful daughter. She will try to like Paris for her mother's sake. She listens patiently both to the nurse's long-winded reminiscences and her mother's artificial speech.

Yet Juliet is not without a maturity of thought despite her youth. She responds obediently to her mother but does not promise to love Paris, saying, *"if looking liking move"*. She has to be asked twice before giving her reply. While she is receptive to finding true love, she is sensible enough not to force the issue.

> *"I'll look to like..."*

LADY CAPULET

Lady Capulet, unlike her husband, shows little consideration for Juliet's own wishes. She is more interested in impressing society by matching Juliet with Paris than in her daughter's own happiness:

> *"Well, think of marriage now; younger than you,*
> *Here in Verona, ladies of esteem,*
> *Are made already mothers:"*

Lady Capulet is ambitious and mercenary in her attitude to marriage. Status and wealth are more important to her than love:

> *"So shall you share all that he doth possess,*
> *By having him making yourself no less."*

THE NURSE

The nurse, by her babbling and witty comments, provides comic relief in a serious situation. By contrast she highlights Lady Capulet's cold seriousness towards her daughter, Juliet:

> *"A man, young lady!...*
> *...why, he's a man of wax."*

The nurse is garrulous and coarse in her speech and often repeats herself. She is, however, a trusted servant in a high position as Juliet's companion.

However, the nurse is an affectionate human woman who loves Juliet dearly and takes great pride in her closeness to Juliet:

> *"Thou wast the prettiest babe that e'er I nursed:*
> *An I might live to see thee married once,*
> *I have my wish."*

Scene IV

The Same. A Street

*Enter Romeo, Mercutio, Benvolio, with five or six
Masquers, Torch-Bearers, and Others*

Romeo

What! shall this speech be spoke for our excuse,
Or shall we on without apology?

Benvolio

The date is out of such prolixity:[1]
We'll have no Cupid hood-wink'd with a scarf,
Bearing a Tartar's painted bow of lath,[2]
Scaring the ladies like a crow-keeper;[3]
Nor no without-book prologue, faintly spoke
After the prompter, for our entrance:
But, let them measure us by what they will,
We'll measure them a measure,[4] and be gone.   10

Romeo

Give me a torch: I am not for this ambling;
Being but heavy, I will bear the light.

Mercutio

Nay, gentle Romeo, we must have you dance.

Romeo

Not I, believe me: you have dancing shoes
With nimble soles; I have a soul of lead   *pun-playonword*
So stakes me to the ground I cannot move.

Mercutio

You are a lover; borrow Cupid's wings,
And soar with them above a common bound.[5]

Romeo

I am too sore enpierced with his shaft
To soar with his light feathers; and so bound   20
I cannot bound a pitch[6] above dull woe:
Under love's heavy burden do I sink.

Mercutio

And, to sink in it, should you burden love;
Too great oppression for a tender thing.

Romeo

Is love a tender thing? it is too rough,
Too rude, too boisterous; and it pricks like thorn.

[1] long-winded speeches are out of fashion

[2] an imitation bow

[3] scarecrow

[4] dance a slow dance

[5] normal limit

[6] height

Mercutio

If love be rough with you, be rough with love;
Prick love for pricking, and you beat love down.
Give me a case[7] to put my visage[8] in:

                   [Putting on a masque

[7]bag
[8]mask

A visor for a visor! what care I,   30
What curious eye doth quote deformities?
Here are the beetle brows[9] shall blush for me.

[9]bushy brows

Benvolio

Come, knock and enter; and no sooner in,
But every man betake him to his legs.

Romeo

A torch for me; let wantons, light of heart,
Tickle the senseless rushes[10] with their heels,
For I am proverb'd with a grandsire phrase;[11]
I'll be a candle-holder, and look on.
The game[12] was ne'er so fair, and I am done.

[10]floor covering
[11]old saying
[12]the dancing

Mercutio

Tut! dun's the mouse,[13] the constable's own word: 40
If thou art Dun, we'll draw thee from the mire,
Or — save your reverence[14] — love, wherein thou
        stick'st
Up to the ears. Come, we burn daylight,[15] ho!

[13]be quiet
[14]forgive the word
[15]delay too long

Romeo

Nay, that's not so.

Mercutio

               I mean, sir, in delay
We waste our lights in vain, like lamps by day.
Take our good meaning for our judgment sits
Five times in that ere once in our five wits.[16]

[16]don't take literally what
    we say

Romeo

And we mean well in going to this masque;
But 'tis no wit to go.

Mercutio

            Why, may one ask?

Romeo

I dream'd a dream to-night.

Mercutio

             And so did I.   50

Romeo

Well, what was yours?

Mercutio

                          That dreamers often lie.

Romeo

In bed asleep, while they do dream things true.

Mercutio

O! then, I see, Queen Mab hath been with you.

Benvolio

Queen Mab! What's she?

Mercutio

She is the fairies' midwife, and she comes
In shape no bigger than an agate-stone
On the fore-finger of an alderman,
Drawn with a team of little atomies[17]
Athwart men's noses as they lie asleep:
Her waggon-spokes made of long spinners'[18] legs;   60
The cover, of the wings of grasshoppers;
The traces, of the smallest spider's web;
The collars, of the moonshine's watery beams;
Her whip, of cricket's bone; the lash, of film;
Her waggoner, a small grey-coated gnat,
Not half so big as a round little worm
Prick'd from the lazy finger of a maid;
Her chariot is an empty hazel-nut,
Made by the joiner squirrel or old grub,
Time out o' mind the fairies' coach-makers.   70
And in this state she gallops night by night
Through lovers' brains, and then they dream of
          love;
O'er courtiers' knees, that dream on curtsies
          straight;
O'er lawyers' fingers, who straight dream on fees;
O'er ladies' lips, who straight on kisses dream;
Which oft the angry Mab with blisters plagues,
Because their breaths with sweetmeats tainted are.
Sometimes she gallops o'er a courtier's nose,
And then dreams he of smelling out a suit;[19]
And sometimes comes she with a tithe-pig's[20] tail,   80
Tickling a parson's nose as a' lies asleep,
Then dreams he of another benefice;
Sometime she driveth o'er a soldier's neck,
And then dreams he of cutting foreign throats,
Of breaches, ambuscadoes,[21] Spanish blades,[22]
Of healths[23] five fathom deep; and then anon

[17]tiny beings

[18]spiders

[19]a favour
[20]a pig given in payment
   of taxes

[21]ambushes
[22]swords
[23]toasts to health

Drums in his ear, at which he starts and wakes;
And, being thus frighted, swears a prayer or two,
And sleeps again. This is that very Mab
That plats the manes of horses in the night;   *90*
And bakes the elf-locks[24] in foul sluttish hairs,   [24]tangles
Which once untangled much misfortune bodes;
This is she —

Romeo
                    Peace, peace! Mercutio, peace!
Thou talk'st of nothing.

Mercutio
                    True, I talk of dreams
Which are the children of an idle brain,
Begot of nothing but vain fantasy;
Which is as thin of substance as the air,
And more inconstant than the wind, who woos
Even now the frozen bosom of the north,
And, being anger'd, puffs away from thence,   *100*
Turning his face to the dew-dropping south.

Benvolio
This wind you talk of blows us from ourselves;
Supper is done, and we shall come too late.

Romeo
I fear too early; for my mind misgives[25]   [25]I am worried
Some consequence yet hanging in the stars
Shall bitterly begin his fearful date
With this night's revels, and expire the term
Of a despised life clos'd in my breast
By some vile forfeit of untimely death.
But he, that hath the steerage of my course,   *110*
Direct my sail! On, lusty gentlemen.

Benvolio
Strike, drum.

                                        [*Exeunt*

Summary – Time: Sunday evening

Mercutio's Wit and Romeo's Premonitions

On a street in Verona, Romeo, Mercutio and Benvolio discuss their plans for entering Capulet's feast as entertainers. Romeo is still sad and wishes to play little part in the merry-making of the others. Mercutio tries to cheer up Romeo by teasing and mocking about love, but Romeo is full of misgivings about their plans. He has an ominous dream. Mercutio, in a long, witty speech, suggests that Queen Mab is responsible for sending man deceiving dreams and fantasies. As Benvolio calls them to enter the feast, Romeo has a sudden premonition that this night's merriment will bring him disaster and death and he appeals to Providence to protect him.

Scene Analysis

Mercutio's Wit

Mercutio's gaiety and lively imagination contrast sharply with Romeo's melancholy and foreboding. Mercutio answers Romeo's serious statements with witty, jocose statements which relieve the seriousness of the scene:

> *"The game was ne'er so fair, and I am done."*   *(Romeo)*

> *"Tut, dun's the mouse, the constable's own word:*
> *If thou art Dun, we'll draw thee from the mire,"*

> *"Or — save your reverence — love, wherein thou stick'st*
> *Up to the ears."*   *(Mercutio)*

Mercutio presents a cold, realistic, even cynical picture of love which contrasts with Romeo's idealistic, romantic view:

> *"True, I talk of dreams,*
> *Which are the children of an idle brain,*
> *Begot of nothing but vain fantasy;"*   *(Mercutio)*

I have a soul of lead
So stakes me to the ground I cannot move.   *(Romeo, Act 1, Scene IV)*

Romeo's Premonitions of Disaster

Romeo's dream and foreboding emphasise the tragic nature of the drama. We are made to feel that not only will disaster arise from the attendance of Romeo at Capulet's ball, but also his *"untimely death"*. Lest we dwell too much on the romantic scenes to follow, Shakespeare prepares us for tragedy:

> *"...for my mind misgives*
> *Some consequence yet hanging in the stars*
> *Shall bitterly begin his fearful date*
> *With this night's revels..."*

Romeo, while he is ready for love at first sight of Juliet, is unwilling to listen to the realism and common sense of Mercutio. So he is the ideal prey of the tragic forces at work in the world of Verona. His idealism and romance must soon come into conflict with the realism and hatred of the world he lives in. He begins to cast himself in the role of a tragic hero without realising it.

Characters

ROMEO

Romeo wishes to be sociable and join in Mercutio's wit and gaiety, but is unable to. He is too oppressed by sadness and depression:

> *"I am too sore enpierced with his shaft*
> *To soar with his light feathers, and so bound..."*

He has *"a soul of lead"* which prevents him from enjoying life.

His love for Rosaline turns him into the world of his imagination and away from the practical world. He is unable to 'pull himself together' as Mercutio advises:

> *"If love be rough with you, be rough with love;*
> *Prick love for pricking, and you beat love down."*

Obviously his love is not real. Only the shock of real love can bring Romeo to his senses later in the play.

MERCUTIO

Mercutio is a loyal friend to Romeo. He tries hard to cheer up Romeo so that he will enjoy the feast. He tries to advise Romeo how to overcome his melancholy. Romeo is unable to listen to this advice:

> *"I talk of dreams...*
> *...Begot of nothing but vain fantasy;"*

Mercutio is witty, sociable and light-hearted. He enjoys playing with words and raising a laugh. Yet he has a serious outlook behind this. He is determined to help his friend, Romeo, to be happy. Mercutio himself has a devil-may-care and cynical attitude to love and life:

> "A visor for a visor! What care I?
> What curious eye doth quote deformities?"

Scene V

The Same. A Hall in Capulet's House

*They march about the Stage and Servingmen
come forth with napkins*

First Servingman
Where's Potpan, that he helps not to take away?
he shift a trencher![1] he scrape a trencher!

Second Servingman
When good manners shall lie all in one or two
men's hands, and they unwashed too, 'tis a foul
thing.

First Servingman
Away with the joint-stools,[2] remove the court-
cupboard,[3] look to the plate. Good thou, save me
a piece of march pane;[4] and, as thou lovest me,
let the porter let in Susan Grindstone and Nell.
Antony! and Potpan!   *10*

Second Servingman
Ay, boy; ready.

First Servingman
You are looked for and called for, asked for and
sought for in the great chamber.

Third Servingman
We cannot be here and there too.

Second Servingman
Cheerly, boys; be brisk awhile, and the longer liver
take all.   *[They retire behind*

*Enter Capulet and Juliet and Others of his house,
meeting the Guests and Masquers*

[1] wooden plate

[2] joined stools
[3] sideboard
[4] marzipan, almond paste

Capulet
Welcome, gentlemen! ladies that have their toes
Unplagu'd with corns will walk a bout⁵ with you.   ⁵dance
Ah ha! my mistresses, which of you all
Will now deny⁶ to dance? she that makes dainty,⁷   ⁶refuse
    she,   20   ⁷hesitates
I'll swear, hath corns; am I come near ye now?
Welcome gentlemen! I have seen the day
That I have worn a visor, and could tell
A whispering tale in a fair lady's ear
Such as would please; 'tis gone, 'tis gone, 'tis
    gone.
You are welcome, gentlemen! Come, musicians,
    play.
A hall! a hall! give room, and foot it, girls.
               [Music plays, and they dance

More light, ye knaves! and turn the tables up,
And quench the fire, the room has grown too hot.
Ah! sirrah, this unlook'd-for sport comes well.   30
Nay, sit, nay, sit, good cousin Capulet,
For you and I are past our dancing days;
How long is 't now since last yourself and I
Were in a mask?⁸   ⁸masque, dance

Second Capulet
        By'r Lady, thirty years.

Capulet
What, man! 'tis not so much, 'tis not so much:
'Tis since the nuptial of Lucentio,
Come Pentecost as quickly as it will,
Some five and twenty years; and then we mask'd.

Second Capulet
'Tis more, 'tis more; his son is elder, sir.
His son is thirty.

Capulet
        Will you tell me that?   40
His son was but a ward two years ago.

Romeo
What lady is that which doth enrich the hand
Of yonder knight?

Servingman
I know not, sir.

Romeo

O! she doth teach the torches to burn bright.
It seems she hangs upon the cheek of night
Like a rich jewel in an Ethiop's ear;
Beauty too rich for use, for earth too dear!
So shows a snowy dove trooping with crows,
As yonder lady o'er her fellows shows.[9]   50
The measure done, I'll watch her place of stand,
And, touching hers, make blessed my rude hand.
Did my heart love till now? forswear it, sight!
For I ne'er saw true beauty till this night.

Tybalt

This, by his voice, should be a Montague.
Fetch me my rapier, boy. What! dares the slave
Come hither, cover'd with an antick face,
To fleer[10] and scorn at our solemnity?
Now, by the stock and honour of my kin,
To strike him dead I hold it not a sin.   60

Capulet

Why, how now, kinsman! wherefore storm you so?

Tybalt

Uncle, this is a Montague, our foe;
A villain that is hither come in spite,
To scorn at our solemnity this night.

Capulet

Young Romeo, is it?

Tybalt

             'Tis he, that villain Romeo.

Capulet

Content thee, gentle coz, let him alone; *he is X having anything*
He bears him like a portly[11] gentleman;
And, to say truth, Verona brags of him
To be a virtuous and well-govern'd youth.
I would not for the wealth of all this town   70
Here in my house do him disparagement;[12]
Therefore be patient, take no note of him:
It is my will; the which if thou respect,
Show a fair presence and put off these frowns,
An ill-beseeming semblance[13] for a feast.

Tybalt

It fits, when such a villain is a guest:
I'll not endure him. *Tybalt went Placal for it*

9 seems

10 to jeer

11 respectable

12 insult

13 conduct

Capulet

                    He shall be endur'd:
What! goodman boy; I say, he shall, go to;
Am I the master here, or you? go to;
You'll not endure him! God shall mend my soul!   80
You'll make a mutiny[14] among my guests!
You will set cock-a-hoop![15] you'll be the man!

[14]disturbance
[15]quarrel

*wants to keep
peace*

Tybalt

Why, uncle, 'tis a shame.

Capulet

                    Go to, go to;
You are a saucy boy — is't so indeed? —
This trick may chance to scathe you. — I
          know what:
You must contrary me! marry, 'tis time.
Well said, my hearts! You are a princox;[16] go:
Be quiet, or — More light, more light! — For
          shame!
I'll make you quiet. What! cheerly, my hearts!

[16]cheeky youth

Tybalt

Patience perforce[17] with wilful choler[18] meeting   90
Makes my flesh tremble in their different greeting.
I will withdraw; but this intrusion shall
Now seeming sweet convert to bitter gall.

[17]enforced
[18]anger

                                              [*Exit*

Romeo [*To Juliet*]

If I profane with my unworthiest hand
This holy shrine, the gentle sin is this;
My lips, two blushing pilgrims, ready stand
To smooth that rough touch with a tender kiss.

Juliet

Good pilgrim, you do wrong your hand too much,
Which mannerly devotion shows in this;
For saints have hands that pilgrims' hands do
          touch,   100
And palm to palm is holy palmers'[19] kiss.

[19]pilgrim

Romeo

Have not saints lips, and holy palmers too?

Juliet

Ay, pilgrim, lips that they must use in prayer.

Romeo

O! then, dear saint, let lips do what hands do;
They pray, grant thou, lest faith turn to despair.

Juliet

Saints do not move, though grant for prayers' sake.

Romeo

Then move not, while my prayers' effect I take.
Thus from my lips, by thine, my sin is purg'd.

[Kissing her

Juliet

Then have my lips the sin that they have took.

Romeo

Sin from my lips? O trespass sweetly urg'd!   *110*
Give me my sin again.

Juliet

                            You kiss by the book.

Nurse

Madam, your mother craves a word with you.

Romeo

What is her mother?

Nurse

                            Marry, bachelor,
Her mother is the lady of the house,
And a good lady, and a wise, and virtuous:
I nurs'd her daughter, that you talk'd withal;
I tell you he that can lay hold of her
Shall have the chinks.[20]

Romeo

                            Is she a Capulet?
O dear account! my life is my foe's debt.

Benvolio

Away, be gone; the sport is at the best.   *120*

Romeo

Ay, so I fear; the more is my unrest.

Capulet

Nay, gentlemen, prepare not to be gone;
We have a trifling foolish banquet towards.[21]
Is it e'en so? Why then, I thank you all;
I thank you, honest gentlemen; good-night.
More torches here! Come on then, let's to bed.

[20]riches

[21]nearly ready

Ah, sirrah, by my fay, it waxes[22] late;
I'll to my rest.   *[Exeunt all except Juliet and Nurse*

[22]is becoming (late)

Juliet
Come hither, nurse. What is yond gentleman?

Nurse
The son and heir of old Tiberio.   *130*

Juliet
What's he that now is going out of door?

Nurse
Marry, that, I think, be young Petruchio.

Juliet
What's he, that follows there, that would not
        dance?

Nurse
I know not.

Juliet
Go, ask his name. — If he be married,
My grave is like to be my wedding bed. — prophetic trace

Nurse
His name is Romeo, and a Montague;
The only son of your great enemy.

Juliet
My only love sprung from my only hate!
Too early seen unknown, and known too late!   *140*
Prodigious[23] birth of love it is to me,
That I must love a loathed enemy.

[23]unlucky, ill-fated

Nurse
What's this, what's this?   *150*

Juliet
                    A rime I learn'd even now
Of one I danc'd withal.   *[One calls within, 'Juliet!'*

Nurse
                    Anon, anon! —
Come, let's away; the strangers are all gone.
                                        [Exeunt

O! she doth teach the torches to burn bright.   *(Romeo, Act 1 Scene V)*

Go ask his name. — If he be married,
My grave is like to be my wedding bed.   *(Juliet, Act 1, Scene V)*

Summary – Time: Sunday evening

The Eventful Dance at Capulet's House

As the servants clear the hall for the dance, Capulet welcomes the masquers who remind him of his own youthful dancing days thirty years earlier.

In the midst of all the hustle and bustle, Romeo notices Juliet and enquires her name. He has fallen in love at first sight of Juliet and realises that he has never truly loved until now.

Tybalt at this moment recognises Romeo as a Montague and feels insulted. Capulet, however, has heard good reports of his uninvited guest and rebukes Tybalt for his lack of hospitality. Tybalt rushes off but vows revenge for this insult.

At this time, Romeo declares his love for Juliet by acting the part of a pilgrim at a shrine of a saint. They have *"exchanged eyes"* and Romeo seeks her permission to kiss her and their love is sealed in this "wooing sonnet".

They separate and Romeo learns that Juliet is a Capulet. All depart except Juliet and the nurse. Juliet discovers that Romeo is a Montague and her happiness in her new-found love is shattered.

Scene Analysis

Reminder of the Feud

In the midst of the comedy of the servants and the merriment at the dance, Tybalt attempts to revive the feud by challenging Romeo to fight:

> "This, by his voice, should be a Montague.
> Fetch me my rapier, boy...
> To strike him dead I hold it not a sin."

A riot is prevented by Capulet, who puts the impetuous Tybalt in his place, since Capulet now desires peace.

However, Tybalt intends to get revenge on Romeo and an outbreak of old rivalries threatens Romeo's new-found love. Thus we are prepared for a crisis, since love and hate, peace and violence vie for supremacy in this scene. Tragic consequences are foreseen by Juliet.

> "My grave is like to be my wedding bed."

The Lovers' Pilgrimage of Love

Romeo's love is "love at first sight", which surpasses any love he has felt up to now. He says of Juliet:

My lips, two blushing pilgrims, ready stand
To smooth that rough touch with a tender kiss.

(Romeo, Act 1, Scene V)

"O, she doth teach the torches to burn bright.
It seems she hangs upon the cheek of night
Like a rich jewel in an Ethiop's ear;
Beauty too rich for use, for earth too dear!"

It is as if Romeo has just come back to life.

Juliet's love is just as sudden:

"Prodigious birth of love it is to me,
That I must love a loathed enemy."

However, Juliet keeps cool and calm while Romeo puts on a romantic display.

Romeo's love is extravagant, idealistic and romantic. His language in wooing Juliet is religious and poetic:

"If I profane with my unworthiest hand
This holy shrine, the gentle sin is this;
My lips, two blushing pilgrims, ready stand
To smooth that rough touch with a tender kiss."

This begins the "wooing sonnet".

Juliet's love is more down-to-earth and realistic. Her language is similar:

"Saints do not move, though grant for prayers' sake."

"You kiss by the book."

Yet she joins Romeo in their declaration of love and is no less sincere than Romeo.

Both have found a love more wonderful than they expected.

Characters

ROMEO

Since we last met him Romeo has come to life and we begin to sympathise more with him. Gone are his melancholy and self-pity. He is a new man:

"Did my heart love till now? forswear it, sight!
For I ne'er saw true beauty till this night."

JULIET

Juliet seemed up to now an obedient, respectful daughter. Now she shows awareness and maturity.

"My only love sprung from my only hate!
Too early seen unknown, and known too late!"

CAPULET

Capulet is a good host, hospitable and considerate of his guests. He confirms for us that he desires peace and an end to the feud. He is determined in his restraining of Tybalt's impetuous outbursts of animosity:

> "I would not for the wealth of all this town
> Here in my house do him disparagement;
> Therefore be patient, take no note of him:"

> "Am I the master here, or you? go to;"

You are welcome, gentlemen! Come musicians, play.
A hall! a hall! give room, and foot it, girls.   (Capulet, Act 1, Scene V)

TYBALT

Tybalt is impetuous and easily provoked to anger. He is spiteful and desires revenge on Romeo for his insulting presence in Capulet's house. Capulet warns that his anger will lead to his downfall:

> "You are a saucy boy— is't so indeed?—
> This trick may chance to scathe you."   (Capulet)

> "I will withdraw; but this intrusion shall
> Now seeming sweet convert to bitter gall."   (Tybalt)

Tybalt intends to precipitate a crisis.

Act 2
Prologue

Enter Chorus

Chorus
Now old desire doth in his death-bed lie,
    And young affection gapes[1] to be his heir;
That fair[2] for which love groan'd for and would die,
    With tender Juliet match'd, is now not fair.
Now Romeo is belov'd and loves again,
    Alike[3] bewitched by the charm of looks,
But to his foe suppos'd he must complain,
    And she steal love's sweet bait from fearful hooks:
Being held a foe, he may not have access
    To breathe such vows as lovers use to[4] swear;
And she as much in love, her means much less
    To meet her new-beloved any where:
But passion lends them power, time means, to meet,
    Tempering extremity with extreme sweet.[5]

                           [Exit

[1] is eager
[2] Rosaline
[3] both
[4] usually
[5] overcoming difficulties with love

Summary
Love Will Overcome Danger

The Chorus summarises the action so far and suggests its future possibilities.

- Romeo's infatuation with Rosaline has given way to *"young affection"* for Juliet.

- Romeo is no longer pining hopelessly: he is loved by Juliet and returns her love.

- However, their love is frustrated by the enmities of their families since they find it difficult to meet safely anywhere.

- Yet the Chorus foretells that *"passion"* will find ways and means to meet, and the sweetness of their love will soften the dangers and threats from the warring world of Verona.

Scene Analysis

This chorus simply confirms what has already happened and hints at the future. Perhaps it is not really necessary at this point in the drama. However, its dramatic purpose seems to be to highlight the context of the growing love relationship. Society and its long-standing

Scene I

Verona. A Lane by the Wall of Capulet's Orchard. Enter Romeo

Romeo

Can I go forward when my heart is here?
Turn back, dull earth, and find thy centre out.

Enter Benvolio and Mercutio

Benvolio

Romeo! my cousin Romeo!

Mercutio

He is wise;
And, on my life, hath stol'n him home to bed.

Benvolio

He ran this way, and leap'd this orchard wall:
Call, good Mercutio.

Mercutio

Nay, I'll conjure[1] too.
Romeo! humours! madman! passion! lover!
Appear thou in the likeness of a sigh:
Speak but one rime and I am satisfied;
Cry but 'Ay me!' pronounce but 'love' and 'dove';   10
Speak to my gossip[2] Venus one fair word.
One nickname for her purblind[3] son and heir,
Young Abraham Cupid,[4] he that shot so trim
When King Cophetua[5] lov'd the beggar-maid.
He heareth not, he stirreth not, he moveth not;
The ape is dead, and I must conjure him.
I conjure thee by Rosaline's bright eyes,
By her high forehead, and her scarlet lip,
By her fine foot, straight leg, and quivering thigh,
That in thy likeness thou appear to us.   20

Benvolio

And if he hear thee, thou wilt anger him.

Mercutio

This cannot anger him: 'twould anger him
To raise a spirit in his mistress' circle
Of some strange nature, letting it there stand
Till she had laid it, and conjur'd it down;
That were some spite: my invocation
Is fair and honest, and in his mistress' name
I conjure only but to raise up him.

[1] use magic

[2] friend
[3] totally blind
[4] character in a ballad
[5] character in a ballad

46

Benvolio

Come, he hath hid himself among these trees,
To be consorted with the humorous night:[6]   *30*
Blind is his love and best befits the dark.

[6] to be close to the moist night

Mercutio

If love be blind, love cannot hit the mark.
Romeo, good night: I'll to my truckle-bed;[7]
This field-bed[8] is too cold for me to sleep:
Come, shall we go?

[7] bed on wheels
[8] camp bed

Benvolio

Go, then; for 'tis in vain
To seek him here that means not to be found.

[Exeunt

Summary – Time: Sunday night directly after Capulet's ball

Romeo Gives his Friends the Slip

Romeo is loath to leave the house where his beloved lives. As Benvolio and Mercutio search for him, he climbs a wall into Capulet's orchard. Mercutio tries to find Romeo by mocking his love for Rosaline. Unable to find Romeo, Mercutio and Benvolio go home without him.

If love be blind, love cannot hit the mark.   (Mercutio, Act 2, Scene I)

Scene Analysis

Escape to Love

This scene continues directly after *Act I Scene V* and allows Romeo to escape from his companions in order to meet Juliet alone. This scene leads directly to the next scene, in which Romeo and Juliet are alone together for the first time.

This scene, through the mockery of Mercutio, allows us to see the hollowness of Romeo's former infatuation with Rosaline. This contrasts with the noble love he now has for Juliet:

> *"I conjure thee by Rosaline's bright eyes,*
> *By her high forehead, and her scarlet lip,"*

and:

> *"Blind is his love and best befits the dark."*

Mercutio's idea of love is merely physical and highlights the purity of the love scene which is to follow directly.

Scene II

The Same. Capulet's Orchard
Enter Romeo

Romeo
He jests at scars, that never felt a wound.

[Juliet appears above at a window

But, soft! what light through yonder window
    breaks?
It is the east, and Juliet is the sun!
Arise, fair sun, and kill the envious moon,
Who is already sick and pale with grief,
That thou her maid art far more fair than she:
Be not her maid, since she is envious;
Her vestal livery[1] is but sick and green,
And none but fools do wear it; cast it off.
It is my lady; O! it is my love: 10
O! that she knew she were.
She speaks, yet she says nothing: what of that?
Her eye discourses;[2] I will answer it.
I am too bold, 'tis not to me she speaks:

[1]virginity

[2]speaks

48

Two of the fairest stars in all the heaven,
Having some business, do entreat her eyes
To twinkle in their spheres till they return.
What if her eyes were there, they in her head?
The brightness of her cheek would shame
        those stars
As daylight doth a lamp; her eyes in heaven   20
Would through the airy region stream so bright
That birds would sing and think it were not night.
See! how she leans her cheek upon her hand:
O! that I were a glove upon that hand,
That I might touch that cheek.

Juliet

              Ay me!

Romeo

                  She speaks;
O! speak again, bright angel; for thou art
As glorious to this night, being o'er my head,
As is a winged messenger of heaven[3]   [3]an angel
Unto the white-upturned wond'ring eyes
Of mortals, that fall back to gaze on him   30
When he bestrides the lazy-pacing clouds,
And sails upon the bosom of the air.

Juliet

O Romeo, Romeo! wherefore art thou Romeo?
Deny thy father, and refuse thy name;
Or, if thou wilt not, be but sworn my love,
And I'll no longer be a Capulet.

Romeo [Aside]

Shall I hear more, or shall I speak at this?

Juliet

'Tis but thy name that is my enemy;
Thou art thyself, though not a Montague.
What's Montague? it is nor hand, nor foot,   40
Nor arm, nor face, nor any other part
Belonging to a man. O! be some other name:
What's in a name? that which we call a rose
By any other name would smell as sweet;
So Romeo would, were he not Romeo call'd,
Retain that dear perfection which he owes[4]   [4]has, owns
Without that title. Romeo, doff thy name;
And for thy name, which is no part of thee,
Take all myself.

Romeo

                I take thee at thy word.
Call me but love, and I'll be new baptiz'd;   *50*
Henceforth I never will be Romeo.

Juliet

What man art thou, that, thus bescreen'd in night,
So stumblest on my counsel?[5]

Romeo

               By a name
I know not how to tell thee who I am:
My name, dear saint, is hateful to myself,
Because it is an enemy to thee:
Had I it written, I would tear the word.

Juliet

My ears have yet not drunk a hundred words
Of that tongue's uttering, yet I know the sound:
Art thou not Romeo, and a Montague?   *60*

Romeo

Neither, fair maid, if either thee dislike.

Juliet

How cam'st thou hither, tell me, and wherefore?
The orchard walls are high and hard to climb,
And the place death, considering who thou art,
If any of my kinsmen find thee here.

Romeo

With love's light wings did I o'erperch[6] these walls;
For stony limits[7] cannot hold love out,
And what love can do that dares love attempt;
Therefore thy kinsmen are no stop[8] to me.

Juliet

If they do see thee they will murder thee.   *70*

Romeo

Alack! there lies more peril in thine eye
Than twenty of their swords: look thou but sweet,
And I am proof[9] against their enmity.

Juliet

I would not for the world they saw thee here.

Romeo

I have night's cloak to hide me from their eyes;
And but thou love me, let them find me here;
My life were better ended by their hate,

Footnotes (left margin):

[5] listen to my thoughts unknown to me

[6] climb over

[7] boundary walls

[8] no hindrance

[9] protected

Than death prorogued,[10] wanting of thy love.

Juliet

By whose direction found'st thou out this place?

Romeo

By Love, that first did prompt me to inquire;   80
He lent me counsel, and I lent him eyes.
I am no pilot; yet, wert thou as far
As that vast shore wash'd with the furthest sea,
I would adventure for such merchandise.

Juliet

Thou know'st the mask of night is on my face,
Else would a maiden blush bepaint[11] my cheek
For that which thou hast heard me speak to-night,
Fain would I dwell on form, fain, fain deny
What I have spoke: but farewell compliment![12]
Dost thou love me? I know thou wilt say 'Ay;'   90
And I will take thy word; yet, if thou swear'st,
Thou mayst prove false; at lovers' perjuries,
They say, Jove laughs. O gentle Romeo!
If thou dost love, pronounce it faithfully:
Or if thou think'st I am too quickly won,
I'll frown and be perverse and say thee nay,
So thou wilt woo; but else, not for the world.
In truth, fair Montague, I am too fond,[13]
And therefore thou mayst think my haviour light:[14]
But trust me, gentleman, I'll prove more true   100
Than those that have more cunning to be strange.[15]
I should have been more strange, I must confess,
But that thou over-heard'st, ere I was 'ware,
My true love's passion: therefore pardon me,
And not impute this yielding to light love,[16]
Which the dark night hath so discovered.[17]

Romeo

Lady, by yonder blessed moon I swear
That tips with silver all these fruit-tree tops, —

Juliet

O! swear not by the moon, the inconstant moon,
That monthly changes in her circled orb,   110
Lest that thy love prove likewise variable.

Romeo

What shall I swear by?

[10]death delayed

[11]cover

[12]formal manners

[13]foolish or affectionate
[14]irresponsible

[15]distant

[16]easily given love
[17]revealed

Juliet

                    Do not swear at all;
Or, if thou wilt, swear by thy gracious self,
Which is the god of my idolatry,
And I'll believe thee.

Romeo

                    If my heart's dear love —

Juliet

Well, do not swear. Although I joy in thee,
I have no joy of this contract to-night:
It is too rash, too unadvis'd, too sudden;
Too like the lightning, which doth cease to be
Ere one can say it lightens. Sweet, good-night!   *120*
This bud of love, by summer's ripening breath,
May prove a beauteous flower when next we meet.
Good-night, good-night! as sweet repose and rest
Come to thy heart as that within my breast!

Romeo

O! wilt thou leave me so unsatisfied?

Juliet

What satisfaction canst thou have to-night?

Romeo

The exchange of thy love's faithful vow for mine.

Juliet

I gave thee mine before thou didst request it;
And yet I would it were to give again.

Romeo

Wouldst thou withdraw it? for what purpose, love?   *130*

Juliet

But to be frank,[18] and give it thee again.
And yet I wish but for the thing I have:
My bounty[19] is as boundless as the sea,
My love as deep; the more I give to thee,
The more I have, for both are infinite.   *[Nurse calls within*
I hear some noise within; dear love, adieu!
Anon, good nurse! Sweet Montague, be true.
Stay but a little, I will come again.   *[Exit above*

Romeo

O blessed, blessed night! I am afeard,
Being in night, all this is but a dream,   *140*
Too flattering-sweet to be substantial.[20]

                              [Re-enter Juliet, above

[18]generous

[19]generosity

[20]real

Juliet
Three words, dear Romeo, and good-night indeed,
If that thy bent of love be honourable,
Thy purpose marriage, send me word to-morrow,
By one that I'll procure[21] to come to thee,   [21]arrange
Where, and what time, thou wilt perform the rite;
And all my fortunes at thy foot I'll lay,
And follow thee my lord throughout the world.

Nurse *[Within]*
Madam.

Juliet
I come, anon. — But if thou mean'st not well.   150
I do beseech thee, —

Nurse *[Within]*
       Madam!

Juliet
       By and by; I come: —
To cease thy suit,[22] and leave me to my grief: [22]put an end to your
To-morrow will I send.   appeals

Romeo
       So thrive my soul, —

Juliet
A thousand times good-night!   *[Exit above*

Romeo
A thousand times the worse, to want thy light.
Love goes toward love, as schoolboys from their
     books;
But love from love, toward school with heavy looks.   *[Retiring*

      Re-enter Juliet, above

Juliet
Hist![23] Romeo, hist! O! for a falconer's voice,   [23]Listen!
To lure this tassel-gentle[24] back again.   [24]male falcon
Bondage is hoarse,[25] and may not speak aloud,   160   [25]love makes me quiet
Else would I tear the cave where Echo[26] lies,   [26]a Roman nymph
And make her airy tongue more hoarse than mine,
With repetition of my Romeo's name.

Romeo
It is my soul that calls upon my name;
How silver-sweet sound lovers' tongues by night,
Like softest music to attending ears!

Juliet
Romeo!

Romeo
                    My dear!
Juliet
                                        At what o'clock tomorrow
Shall I send to thee?
Romeo
                    At the hour of nine.
Juliet
I will not fail; 'tis twenty years till then.
I have forgot why I did call thee back.   170
Romeo
Let me stand here till thou remember it.
Juliet
I shall forget, to have thee still stand there,
Remembering how I love thy company.
Romeo
And I'll still stay, to have thee still forget,
Forgetting any other home but this.
Juliet
'Tis almost morning; I would have thee gone;
And yet no further than a wanton's[27] bird,
Who lets it hop a little from her hand,
Like a poor prisoner in his twisted gyves,[28]
And with a silk thread plucks it back again,   180
So loving-jealous of his liberty.
Romeo
I would I were thy bird.
Juliet
                    Sweet, so would I:
Yet I should kill thee with much cherishing.
Good-night, good-night! parting is such sweet
          sorrow
That I shall say good-night till it be morrow.   [Exit
Romeo
Sleep dwell upon thine eyes, peace in thy breast!
Would I were sleep and peace, so sweet to rest!
Hence will I to my ghostly[29] father's cell,
His help to crave, and my dear hap[30] to tell.   [Exit

[27]an irresponsible girl

[28]fetters, ties

[29]spiritual

[30]good fortune

Summary – Time: Sunday night directly after Act 2, Scene I to dawn Monday morning

The Love Scene in Capulet's Garden

Romeo rejects Mercutio's mockery and notices Juliet on her balcony overlooking the garden. In a soliloquy, Romeo worships the beauty of his new love Juliet in extravagant comparisons to the sun, the stars and an angel of heaven.

Juliet is unaware of Romeo's presence and confesses that she truly loves Romeo. She laments that their social positions must keep them apart. She is willing to disown her name and family to be Romeo's love.

At this moment, Romeo reveals his presence and declares that he too will abandon his name and family for love of Juliet. Juliet is concerned for the danger to Romeo's life by his presence in his enemy's garden, but Romeo would rather die than be without her love and would pursue her to the *"furthest sea"*. Juliet is embarrassed that Romeo has heard her declare her love so openly.

Recovering her composure, Juliet promises that her love will be just as true as if it had been less easily won. She wishes Romeo to swear by his *"gracious self"* to be her true love.

Juliet then interrupts Romeo's declaration to warn him of the danger of rushing into things and hopes for fulfilment of their love when next they meet. Romeo wished to exchange their vows of love before they part. Then Juliet declares how deeply she loves Romeo. Romeo wonders if he is in a dream.

The nurse calls Juliet and as she returns she makes practical plans for their marriage. Romeo is to make arrangements and send her word the next day. The nurse calls again and Juliet leaves Romeo, who is unwilling to go. Juliet returns immediately, not wishing to be parted from Romeo. Eventually they part lovingly and Romeo goes straight away to seek Friar Laurence's help.

Scene Analysis

A Moment of True Happiness and Beauty

This famous scene captures the atmosphere of romance. It is night time and the moon and stars light up the first meeting of the lovers alone. It is as if the night itself is in sympathy with the lovers, protecting their love.

In this scene, the depth and intensity of the love of Romeo and Juliet become clear.

Romeo is totally committed to his love and nothing else matters:

> *"It is my lady; O! it is my love:*
> *O! that she knew she were."*

How silver-sweet sound lovers' tongues by night,
Like softest music to attending ears!

(Romeo, Act 2, Scene II)

and

> "The brightness of her cheek would shame those stars
> As daylight doth a lamp;"

Juliet is more practical, but loves Romeo deeply and openly:

> "My bounty is as boundless as the sea,
> My love as deep; the more I give to thee,
> The more I have, for both are infinite."

What's in a name? that which we call a rose
By any other name would smell as sweet;   (Juliet, Act 2, Scene II)

Their love is like light in the darkness or sweet music:

> "How silver-sweet sound lovers' tongues by night,
> Like softest music to attending ears!"

A Moment of Isolation

The light of true love is isolated from the darkness of a hate-filled society in this scene. For a brief moment, the lovers are allowed to enjoy their exchanges of love, uninterrupted by the demands of an unsympathetic society. Their love blossoms in this idyllic night-time context away from the conflicts of the day time.

However, that hostile world is never far from Juliet's mind. Romeo can escape to the poetic world of sun, moon and stars, but Juliet is conscious of the vulnerability of their love at the hands of her kinsmen:

> *"And the place death, considering who thou art,*
> *If any of my kinsmen find thee here."*

Romeo can dismiss the dangers lightly:

> *"And I am the proof against their enmity."*

But Juliet has premonitions of disaster:

> *"...although I joy in thee,*
> *I have no joy of this contract to-night:*
> *It is too rash, too unadvis'd, too sudden."*

At the conclusion of the scene Romeo wishes:

> *"Would I were sleep and peace, so sweet to rest!"*

We are reminded, even in the beautiful love scene, not to expect a fairy-tale ending to the drama. The lovers are all alone against a hostile world. Tragedy will be the result.

Characters

ROMEO

Romeo is more impractical than Juliet, but there is no doubt of the reality of his love for Juliet. He declares his love in imaginative terms:

> *"It is the east, and Juliet is the sun!*
> *Arise, fair sun, and kill the envious moon,"*

Yet he is prepared to sacrifice all for his love, if necessary:

> *"Call me but love, and I'll be new baptiz'd;*
> *Henceforth I never will be Romeo."*

He has begun to change from the melancholy, anti-social lover of *Act 1 Scene I*. Romeo is no longer passive and dreamy, but is more decisive and courageous than before. He says:

> *"...thy kinsmen are no stop to me."*

and:

> *"My life were better ended by their hate,*
> *Than death prorogued, wanting of thy love."*

He gains our admiration and sympathy.

JULIET

Juliet is more realistic and practical than Romeo. She realises the danger of Romeo's presence in her father's orchard and of rushing into marriage too hastily. She is more conscious of the values of society than Romeo. She blushes for declaring her love so freely and openly, since she is a woman. But it is the strength of her love which prompts her to abandon conventional standards:

"But trust me, gentleman, I'll prove more true
"Than those that have more cunning to be strange."

Juliet is sincere and passionate, wholehearted and determined in her love. She is prepared to sacrifice herself totally for love of Romeo. She promises fidelity and expects the same from Romeo in return:

"My bounty is as boundless as the sea,
My love as deep; the more I give to thee,
The more I have, for both are infinite."

and:

"And all my fortunes at thy foot I'll lay,
And follow thee my lord throughout the world."

Scene III

The Same. Friar Laurence's Cell
Enter Friar Laurence, with a basket

Friar Laurence
The grey-ey'd morn smiles on the frowning night,
Chequering the eastern clouds with streaks of
          light,
And fleckled darkness like a drunkard reels
From forth day's path and Titan's[1] fiery wheels:
Now, ere the sun advance his burning eye
The day to cheer and night's dank dew to dry,
I must up-fill this osier cage[2] of ours
With baleful[3] weeds and precious-juiced flowers.
The earth that's nature's mother is her tomb;
What is her burying grave that is her womb,   10
And from her womb children of divers kind
We sucking on her natural bosom find,
Many for many virtues[4] excellent,
None but for some, and yet all different.
O! mickle[5] is the powerful grace that lies
In herbs, plants, stones, and their true qualities:
For nought so vile that on the earth doth live
But to the earth some special good doth give,
Nor aught so good but strain'd[6] from that fair use

[1] the sun-god

[2] willow basket
[3] poisonous

[4] powers

[5] great

[6] diverted away

7 turns away from its true purpose
8 when wrongly used

Revolts from true birth,[7] stumbling on abuse;[8]   20
Virtue itself turns vice, being misapplied,
And vice sometimes by action dignified.

Enter Romeo

9 seedling stalk/skin

Within the infant rind[9] of this weak flower
Poison hath residence and medicine power:
For this, being smelt, with that part cheers each
          part; [10]

10 stimulates each part of the body

Being tasted, slays all senses with the heart.
Two such opposed kings encamp them still
In man as well as herbs, grace and rude will;
And where the worser is predominant,

11 destructive

Full soon the canker[11] death eats up that plant.   30

Romeo

Good morrow, father!

Friar Laurence

12 bless you

Benedicite![12]
What early tongue so sweet saluteth me?

13 disturbed mind

Young son, it argues a distemper'd head[13]
So soon to bid good morrow to thy bed:
Care keeps his watch in every old man's eye,
And where care lodges, sleep will never lie;

14 untroubled
15 rest

But where unbruised youth with unstuff'd brain[14]
Doth couch[15] his limbs, there golden sleep doth
          reign:
Therefore thy earliness doth me assure
Thou art up-rous'd by some distemperature;   40
Or if not so, then here I hit it right,
Our Romeo hath not been in bed to-night.

Romeo

That last is true; the sweeter rest was mine.

Friar Laurence

God pardon sin! wast thou with Rosaline?

Romeo

With Rosaline, my ghostly father? no;
I have forgot that name, and that name's woe.

Friar Laurence

That's my good son: but where hast thou been
          then?

Romeo

I'll tell thee, ere thou ask it me again.
I have been feasting with mine enemy,
Where on a sudden one hath wounded me,   50

That's by me wounded: both our remedies
Within thy help and holy physic[16] lies:
I bear no hatred, blessed man; for, lo!
My intercession[17] likewise steads[18] my foe.

Friar Laurence

Be plain, good son, and homely[19] in thy drift;
Riddling confession finds but riddling shrift.[20]

Romeo

Then plainly know my heart's dear love is set
On the fair daughter of rich Capulet:
As mine on hers, so hers is set on mine;
And all combin'd, save what thou must combine   60
By holy marriage: when and where and how
We met, we woo'd and made exchange of vow,
I'll tell thee as we pass; but this I pray,
That thou consent to marry us to-day.

Friar Laurence

Holy Saint Francis! what a change is here;
Is Rosaline, whom thou didst love so dear,
So soon forsaken? young men's love then lies
Not truly in their hearts, but in their eyes.
Jesu Maria! what a deal of brine
Hath wash'd thy sallow cheeks for Rosaline;   70
How much salt water thrown away in waste,
To season[21] love, that of it doth not taste!
The sun not yet thy sighs from heaven clears,
Thy old groans ring yet in my ancient ears;
Lo! here upon thy cheek the stain doth sit
Of an old tear that is not wash'd off yet.
If e'er thou wast thyself and these woes thine,
Thou and these woes were all for Rosaline:
And art thou chang'd? pronounce this sentence
          then:
Women may fall, when there's no strength in men.   80

Romeo

Thou chidd'st me oft for loving Rosaline.

Friar Laurence

For doting, not for loving, pupil mine.

Romeo

And bad'st me bury love.

Friar Laurence

                    Not in a grave,
To lay one in, another out to have.

16 medicine

17 appeal
18 helps

19 clear
20 forgiveness

21 preserve, flavour

Romeo
I pray thee, chide not; she, whom I love now
Doth grace for grace and love for love allow;
The other did not so.

Friar Laurence
                              O! she knew well

²²said without meaning
   what you said

Thy love did read by rote²² that could not spell.
But come, young waverer, come, go with me,
In one respect I'll thy assistant be;   90
For this alliance may so happy prove,
To turn your households' rancour to pure love.

Romeo
O! let us hence; I stand on sudden haste.

Friar Laurence
Wisely and slow; they stumble that run
                    fast.   [Exeunt

Summary – Time: Early on Monday morning directly after Act 2, Scene II

An Eager Helper for Romeo

Friar Laurence is gathering herbs to make medicine, for he is skilled in making poisons. He moralises in a long soliloquy that good and evil, love and hate are present together in the world and it depends on man himself which of these will get the upper hand. In this world excess of passion will bring death.

The friar's long-winded questions elicit that Romeo is no longer captivated by Rosaline but is in love with his enemy's daughter. The friar is surprised at this sudden change in Romeo's affections, but is glad that Romeo is no longer *"doting"*.

Romeo appeals to the friar to marry them this very day. The friar consents to help since he sees an opportunity to bring love and harmony to the rancour of the hostile families. However, he warns Romeo not to be too hasty lest he bring misfortune on himself.

Scene Analysis

Marriage Plans

In the cool of the morning, the passionate confessions of love of the previous scene are brought a step nearer to fulfilment – plans are made for an early marriage. Romeo has no second thoughts about the advisability of marrying his enemy's only daughter. The plot of the drama advances quickly in the scene.

While the friar's *"grace"* contrasts with Romeo's *"rude will"* or passion, the friar very hastily agrees to marry Romeo and Juliet. Perhaps the justification is his concern for his protégé, Romeo, or perhaps it is his zeal for peace in hate-ridden Verona. Ironically, he advises Romeo not to be hasty.

We met, we woo'd and made exchange of vow,
I'll tell thee as we pass; but this I pray,
That thou consent to marry us to-day.   (Romeo, Act 2, Scene III)

Characters

ROMEO

Romeo shows us that he meant his declaration of fidelity given to Juliet. He is true to his love and his motives are sincere and honourable, unlike his previous moodiness over his frustrated love of Rosaline:

> *"Then plainly know my heart's dear love is set*
> *On the fair daughter of rich Capulet:*
> *As mine on hers, so hers is set on mine;*
> *And all combin'd...*
> *By holy marriage:"*

Romeo impresses us by his decisive actions and determination to fulfil his promise of marriage.

> *"That thou consent to marry us to-day."*

and

> *"I stand on sudden haste."*

This is not impetuousity but a sincere determination to fulfil of his promise.

FRIAR LAURENCE

Friar Laurence is a deep thinker and is knowledgeable on herbs and medicines. He is gathering herbs and moralising when Romeo enters:

> *"Virtue itself turns vice, being misapplied;*
> *And vice sometimes by action dignified."*

He is a holy and spiritual man who believes in practical charity. He is Romeo's confidant and is almost too eager to help. He is zealous for peace in the world of Verona:

> *"In one respect I'll thy assistant be...*
> *To turn your households' rancour to pure love."*

Although he is sincere, he is not very sensible in helping Romeo to marry secretly and illegally.

Scene IV

The Same. A Street. Enter Benvolio and Mercutio

Mercutio
Where the devil should this Romeo be?
Came he not home to-night?

Benvolio
Not to his father's; I spoke with his man.

Mercutio
Why that same pale hard-hearted wench, that
        Rosaline,
Torments him so, that he will sure run mad.

Benvolio
Tybalt, the kinsman of old Capulet,
Hath sent a letter to his father's house.

Mercutio
A challenge, on my life.

Benvolio

Romeo will answer it.

Mercutio

Any man that can write may answer a letter.   *10*

Benvolio

Nay, he will answer the letter's master, how he
dares, being dared.

Mercutio

Alas! poor Romeo, he is already dead; stabbed
with a white wench's black eye; run through the ear
with a love-song; the very pin[1] of his heart   [1] centre
cleft with the blind bow-boy's butt-shaft;[2] and is he   [2] Cupid's blunt arrow
a man to encounter Tybalt?

Benvolio

Why, what is Tybalt?

Mercutio

More than prince of cats, I can tell you. O! he is
the courageous captain of compliments.[3] He   *20*   [3] formalities
fights as you sing prick-song,[4] keeps time,   [4] music written down
distance, and proportion; rests me his minim[5] rest,   [5] shortest
one, two, and the third in your bosom; the very
butcher of a silk button, a duellist, a duellist; a
gentleman of the very first house,[6] of the first and   [6] first place
second cause.[7] Ah! the immortal passado![8] the   [7] grounds for taking offence
punto reverso![9] the hay![10]   and giving challenge in a
                                                                   duel
                                                               [8] lunge
                                                               [9] backhanded strike
                                                               [10] hit
Benvolio

The what?

Mercutio

The pox of such antick, lisping, affecting fantast-
icoes[11] these new tuners of accents! — 'By   *30*   [11] would-be gallant
Jesu, a very good blade! — a very tall man! a very   gentlemen
good whore'. — Why, is not this a lamentable thing,
grandsire, that we should be thus afflicted with
these strange flies, these fashion-mongers,
these pardon-mees,[12] who stand so much on the   [12] fops, show-offs
new form that they cannot sit at ease on the old
bench? O, their bones, their bones!

Enter Romeo

Benvolio

Here comes Romeo, here comes Romeo.

[13]Italian love poet
[14]The subject of Petrarch's sonnets
[15]Queen of Carthage who was hopelessly in love with Aeneas
[16]Queen of Egypt who poisoned herself for love of Antony
[17]loved Paris and caused siege of Troy
[18]swam the Hellespont to see his love, Leander
[19]harlots
[20]loved Pyramus (tragically)
[21]loose trousers
[22]slip
[23]remember

Mercutio

Without his roe, like a dried herring. O flesh, flesh,
how art thou fishified! Now is he for the numbers   40
that Petrarch[13] flowed in: Laura[14] to his lady was but a
kitchen-wench; marry, she had a better love to
be-rime her; Dido[15] a dowdy; Cleopatra[16] a gipsy;
Helen[17] and Hero[18] hildings[19] and harlots; Thisbe,[20] a grey
eye or so, but not to the purpose. Signior
Romeo, *bon jour!* there's a French salutation
to your French slop.[21] You gave us the counterfeit[22]
fairly last night.

Romeo

Good morrow to you both. What counterfeit did
I give you?   50

Mercutio

The slip, sir, the slip; can you not conceive?[23]

Romeo

Pardon, good Mercutio, my business was great;
and in such a case as mine a man may strain
courtesy.

Mercutio

That's as much as to say, such a case as yours
constrains a man to bow in the hams.

Romeo

Meaning — to curtsy.

Mercutio

Thou has most kindly hit it.

Romeo

A most courteous exposition.

Mercutio

Nay, I am the very pink of courtesy.   60

Romeo

Pink for flower.

Mercutio

Right.

Romeo

Why, then, is my pump[24] well flowered.

Mercutio

Sure wit! follow me this jest now till thou hast worn
out the pump, that, when the single sole of it is
worn, the jest may remain after the wearing sole
singular.

[24]shoe

Romeo

O single-soled jest! solely singular for the
singleness.

Mercutio

Come between us, good Benvolio; my wit faints.   *70*

Romeo

Switch and spurs, switch and spurs; or I'll cry a
match.

Mercutio

Nay, if thy wits run the wild-goose chase, I have
done, for thou hast more of the wild-goose in one
of thy wits than, I am sure, I have in my whole five.
Was I with you there for the goose?

Romeo

Thou wast never with me for anything when thou
wast not there for the goose.

Mercutio

I will bite thee by the ear for that jest.

Romeo

Nay, good goose, bite not.   *80*

Mercutio

Thy wit is a very bitter sweeting; it is a most sharp
sauce.

Romeo

And is it not then well served in to a sweet goose?

Mercutio

O! here's a wit of cheveril,[25] that stretches from
an inch narrow to an ell broad.[26]

[25]a great wit

[26]forty-five inches wide

Romeo

I stretch it out for that word 'broad'; which added
to the goose, proves thee far and wide a broad
goose.[27]

[27]indecent goose

Mercutio

Why, is this not better now than groaning for love?
now art thou sociable, now art thou Romeo; now   *90*
art thou what thou art, by art as well as by nature:
for this drivelling love is like a great natural,[28]
that runs lolling up and down to hide his bauble[29]
in a hole.

[28]fool

[29]trinket

Benvolio

Stop there, stop there.

Mercutio

Thou desirest me to stop in my tale against the
hair.[30]

Benvolio

Thou wouldst else have made thy tale large.[31]

Mercutio

O! thou art deceived; I would have made it short;
for I was come to the whole depth of my tale, and   100
meant indeed to occupy the argument no longer.

Romeo

Here's goodly gear!

Enter Nurse and Peter

A sail, a sail!

Mercutio

Two, two; a shirt and a smock.[32]

Nurse

Peter!

Peter

Anon!

Nurse

My fan, Peter.

Mercutio

Good Peter, to hide her face; for her fan's the fairer
face.

Nurse

God ye good morrow, gentlemen.   110

Mercutio

God ye good den, fair gentlewoman.

Nurse

Is it good den?

Mercutio

'Tis no less, I tell you; for the hand of the dial is
now upon the prick of noon.

Nurse

Out upon you! what a man are you?

Romeo

One, gentlewoman, that God hath made for himself
to mar.

31 indecent

32 a man and a woman

Nurse
By my troth, it is well said; 'for himself to mar,'
quoth a'? — Gentleman, can any of you tell me
where I may find the young Romeo?   *120*

Romeo
I can tell you; but young Romeo will be older when
you have found him than he was when you sought
him: I am the youngest of that name, for fault of a worse.

Nurse
You say well.

Mercutio
Yea! is the worst well? very well took, i' faith;
wisely, wisely.

Nurse
If you be he, sir, I desire some confidence with you.

Benvolio
She will indite[33] him to some supper.   [33]invite

Mercutio
A bawd, a bawd, a bawd! So ho!

Romeo
What hast thou found?   *130*

Mercutio
No hare, sir; unless a hare, sir, in a lenten pie, that
is something stale and hoar ere it be spent.
Romeo, will you come to your father's? we'll to
dinner thither.

Romeo
I will follow you.

Mercutio
Farewell, ancient lady; farewell,
[Singing] 'Lady, lady, lady.'
                                  [Exeunt Mercutio and Benvolio

Nurse
Marry, farewell! I pray you, sir, what saucy
merchant was this, that was so full of his ropery?[34]

                                                                    [34]roguish talk
Romeo
A gentleman, nurse, that loves to hear himself talk,   *140*
and will speak more in a minute than he will stand
to in a month.

Nurse

An a'speak anything against me, I'll take him down,
an a' were lustier than he is, and twenty such
Jacks; and if I cannot, I'll find those that shall.
Scurvy knave! I am none of his flirt-gills;[35]
I am none of his skeins-mates.[36] *[To Peter]* And
thou must stand by too, and suffer every knave to
use me at his pleasure!

Peter

I saw no man use you at his pleasure; if I had, my   150
weapon should quickly have been out, I warrant
you. I dare draw as soon as another man, if I see
occasion in a good quarrel, and the law on my side.

Nurse

Now, afore God, I am so vexed, that every part
about me quivers. Scurvy knave! Pray you, sir, a
word; and as I told you, my young lady bid me
inquire you out; what she bid me say I will keep to
myself; but first let me tell ye, if ye should lead
her into a fool's paradise,[37] as they say, it were
a very gross kind of behaviour, as they say: for   160
the gentlewoman is young; and, therefore, if you
should deal doubly with her, truly it were an ill
thing to be offered to any gentlewoman, and very
weak[38] dealing.

Romeo

Nurse, commend me to thy lady and mistress.
I protest unto thee, —

Nurse

Good heart! and, i' faith, I will tell her as much.
Lord, Lord! she will be a joyful woman.

Romeo

What wilt thou tell her, nurse? thou dost not
mark me.   170

Nurse

I will tell her, sir, that you do protest; which, as I
take it, is a gentlemanlike offer.

Romeo

Bid her devise
Some means to come to shrift this afternoon;
And there she shall at Friar Laurence' cell,
Be shriv'd and married. Here is for thy pains.

[35]flirting women
[36]harlots

[37]seduction

[38]unmanly

Nurse running rings round Romeo / not Juliet. Juliet anything else

arrangement for marriage

Nurse

No, truly, sir; not a penny.

Romeo

Go to; I say, you shall.

Nurse

This afternoon, sir? well, she shall be there.

Romeo

And stay, good nurse, behind the abbey wall: *180*
Within this hour my man shall be with thee,
And bring thee cords made like a tackled stair;[39]   [39]rope ladder
Which to the high top-gallant[40] of my joy   [40]summit
Must be my convoy[41] in the secret night.   [41]conveyance
Farewell! Be trusty, and I'll quit thy pains.[42]   [42]pay you for the trouble
Farewell! Commend me to thy mistress.

Nurse

Now God in heaven bless thee! Hark you, sir.

Romeo

What sayest thou, my dear nurse?

Nurse

Is your man secret? Did you ne'er hear say
Two may keep counsel, putting one away?   *190*

Romeo

I warrant thee my man's as true as steel.

Nurse

Well, sir; my mistress is the sweetest lady — Lord,
Lord! — when 'twas a little prating thing, — O!
there's a nobleman in town, one Paris, that would
fain lay knife aboard; but she, good soul, had as lief
see[43] a toad, a very toad, as see him. I anger her   [43]prefer to see
sometimes and tell her that Paris is the properer
man; but, I'll warrant you, when I say so, she looks
as pale as any clout in the versal world.[44] Doth   [44]cloth in the universe
not rosemary and Romeo begin both with a letter?   *200*

Romeo

Ay, nurse: what of that? both with an R.

Nurse

Ah! mocker; that's the dog's name. R is for the —
No; I know it begins with some other letter: and
she had the prettiest sententious[45] of it, of you   [45]sentences
and rosemary, that it would do you good to hear it.

Romeo

Commend me to thy lady.

Nurse

Ay, a thousand times. *[Exit Romeo]* Peter!

Peter

Anon!

Nurse

⁴⁶quickly

Before, and apace.⁴⁶   *[Exeunt*

Summary – Time: At Midday on Monday

Tybalt's Challenge and Romeo's Plans

Benvolio and Mercutio are still searching for Romeo on Monday. Tybalt has carried out his threat and has issued a challenge to the Montagues which Benvolio believes Romeo will accept despite the slim hope of his winning.

Romeo meets his friends, and, to their surprise, joins in their witty exchanges and sexual innuendos. Romeo is a new man; he is in high spirits and sociable.

The nurse comes as Juliet's messenger to meet Romeo, and her arrival leads to more jesting and horseplay at her expense. She pretends to be offended by Mercutio's insinuations, but enjoys the opportunity to engage in vulgar and common jesting.

Mercutio and Benvolio leave and Romeo discusses his plans for marriage. Juliet is to make excuses and come to Friar Laurence's cell that evening to be married. Romeo will send a rope-ladder to the nurse so that he can be with Juliet that night. The nurse agrees and they part. All is arranged for the marriage and the wedding night.

Scene Analysis

Romeo's Plans are Threatened

The play is gradually developing towards the climax in *Act 3 Scene I*. Romeo and Juliet are about to be married and we hope their marriage will be happy. Yet the spiteful Tybalt has issued a challenge to the Montagues which, in honour, Romeo must answer. His chances of defeating Tybalt are slim since Tybalt is a formidable adversary. Love and hate yet again come into conflict and Romeo's happiness in marriage seems short-lived.

Comic Relief from the Impending Tragedy

The play so far has been serious and intense. In this scene Mercutio and the nurse counter-balance our sense of inevitable doom by their vulgar and witty exchanges:

    "A sail, a sail!"   (Mercutio)

    "Two, two; a shirt and a smock."   (Benvolio)

Romeo and Mercutio were earlier in high spirits:

> *"...now art thou sociable, now art thou Romeo; now*
> *art thou what thou art, by art as well as by nature:"*

The gaiety and laughter of the scene relieve the tension caused by Tybalt's challenge and Romeo's hasty plans for marriage, despite the increasing danger he is in.

Tybalt, the kinsman of old Capulet,
Hath sent a letter to his father's house.   *(Benvolio, Act 2, Scene IV)*

Characters

ROMEO

Romeo shows his witty, sociable side in this scene, despite his preoccupation with making plans for his marriage. He says of Mercutio:

> "A gentleman, nurse, that loves to hear himself talk,
> and will speak more in a minute than he will stand
> to in a month."

MERCUTIO

Mercutio is naturally sociable and witty. His wit is more subtle than the nurse's which is common gossip. He jokes with serious intention to expose the vices or follies of others. In disgust, he says of Tybalt:

> "More, than prince of cats, I can tell you. O! he
> is the courageous captain of compliments."

Mercutio is a loyal friend to Romeo and much of his wit is aimed at cheering up Romeo from his melancholy state of mind (as Mercutio thinks). He is delighted to realise that Romeo has already overcome his depression:

> "Why, is this not better now than groaning for love?"

THE NURSE

The nurse is full of her own importance. She revels in delivering important messages and enjoys ordering Peter and displaying her fan, a sign of her position in the Capulet household.

She is talkative and enjoys garrulous and common talk. She readily joins in the vulgar jesting at her expense:

> "An a 'speak anything against me, I'll take him down,
> an a' were lustier than he is, and twenty such
> Jacks;"

Yet she is trusted by Juliet in this important errand. Nothing diverts her from her purpose. She accepts money when persuaded by Romeo, but is concerned for the secrecy of Juliet and Romeo's plans:

> "Is your man secret? Did you ne'er hear say
> Two may keep counsel, putting one away?"

Scene V

The Same. Capulet's Garden. Enter Juliet

Juliet

The clock struck nine when I did send the nurse;
In half an hour she promis'd to return.
Perchance she cannot meet him: that's not so.
O! she is lame: love's heralds should be thoughts,
Which ten times faster glide than the sun's beams,
Driving back shadows over lowering hills:
Therefore do nimble-pinion'd[1] doves draw Love,   [1]swift-winged
And therefore hath the wind-swift Cupid wings.
Now is the sun upon the highmost hill
Of this day's journey, and from nine till twelve   10
Is three long hours, yet she is not come.
Had she affections, and warm youthful blood,
She'd be as swift in motion as a ball;
My words would bandy her[2] to my sweet love,   [2]hurry her
And his to me:
But old folks, many feign[3] as they were dead;   [3]pretend, act
Unwieldy, slow, heavy and pale as lead.

Enter Nurse and Peter

O God! she comes. O honey nurse! what news?
Hast thou met with him? Send thy man away.

Nurse

Peter, stay at the gate.   [*Exit Peter* 20

Juliet

Now, good sweet nurse; O Lord! why look'st
    thou sad?
Though news be sad, yet tell them merrily;
If good, thou sham'st the music of sweet news
By playing it to me with so sour a face.

Nurse

I am aweary, give me leave awhile:
Fie, how my bones ache! What a jaunce[4] have I   [4]journey, walk
    had!

Juliet

I would thou hadst my bones, and I thy news.
Nay, come, I pray thee, speak; good, good nurse,
    speak.

⁵wait

Nurse

Jesu! what haste? can you not stay⁵ awhile?

Do you not see that I am out of breath?   30

Juliet

How art thou out of breath when thou hast breath

To say to me that thou art out of breath?

The excuse that thou dost make in this delay

Is longer than the tale thou dost excuse.

Is thy news good, or bad? answer to that;

⁶details

Say either, and I'll stay the circumstance:⁶

Let me be satisfied, is't good or bad?

Nurse

⁷foolish

Well, you have made a simple⁷ choice; you know

not how to choose a man: Romeo! no, not he;

though his face be better than any man's, yet his   40

leg excels all men's; and for a hand, and a foot, and

a body, though they be not to be talked on, yet

they are past compare. He is not the flower of

courtesy, but, I'll warrant him, as gentle as a lamb.

Go thy ways, wench; serve God. What! have you

dined at home?

Juliet

No, no: but all this did I know before.

What says he of our marriage? what of that?

Nurse

Lord! how my head aches; what a head have I!

It beats as it would fall in twenty pieces.   50

My back o' t'other side; O! my back, my back!

⁸curse

Beshrew⁸ your heart for sending me about,

To catch my death with jauncing up and down.

Juliet

I'faith, I am sorry that thou art not well.

Sweet, sweet, sweet nurse, tell me, what says my

    love?

Nurse

Your love says, like an honest gentleman, and a

courteous, and a kind, and a handsome, and, I

warrant, a virtuous, — Where is your mother?

Juliet

Where is my mother! why, she is within;

Where should she be? How oddly thou repliest: 60

'Your love says, like an honest gentleman,

Where is your mother?'

Nurse
                    O! God's lady dear,
Are you so hot?[9] Marry, come up, I trow;
Is this the poultice for my aching bones?
Henceforward do your messages yourself.

Juliet
Here's such a coil![10] come, what says Romeo?

Nurse
Have you got leave to go to shrift to-day?

Juliet
I have.

Nurse
Then hie you hence to Friar Laurence's cell,
There stays a husband to make you a wife: *70*
Now comes the wanton blood up in your cheeks,
They'll be in scarlet straight[11] at any news.
Hie[12] you to church; I must another way,
To fetch a ladder, by the which your love
Must climb a bird's nest soon when it is dark;
I am the drudge and toil in your delight,
But you shall bear the burden soon at night.
Go; I'll to dinner: hie you to the cell.

Juliet
Hie to high fortune! Honest nurse, farewell.   *80*
                            [Exeunt

[9] angry

[10] confusion

[11] straightaway
[12] go

Summary – Time: Early on Monday afternoon directly after Act 2, Scene IV

Juliet Awaits Romeo's Message

The scene begins with Juliet in the garden anxiously awaiting the nurse's return with news of Romeo's plans for their wedding. The nurse is late and Juliet rationalises that the old are slower than the young.

At last the nurse arrives but she looks sad and complains of weariness. Juliet is eager for definite news, but the nurse teases her by both praising and mocking Romeo. Juliet sympathises with the nurse's tiredness, but the nurse still delays in conveying news of Romeo.

When Juliet becomes angry, the nurse puts an end to the suspense and tells the impatient Juliet of the plans. Juliet must go to Friar Laurence that afternoon to be married. The nurse will fetch the ladder so that Romeo can climb into Juliet's room that night. Juliet is relieved and delighted.

Scene Analysis

Juliet's Determination

This scene tests Juliet's resolve to marry Romeo. Her soliloquy shows how real her love is. She is faithful to her promises:

> *"O! she is lame: love's heralds should be thoughts,*
> *Which ten times faster glide than the sun's beams,"*

The nurse's delaying tactics emphasise how eager Juliet is to marry Romeo:

> *"Sweet, sweet, sweet nurse, tell me, what says my love?"*

The suspense caused by the nurse in delivering a simple message delays the forward progress of the play and creates anxiety and sympathy for Juliet in the audience. The finalising of the marriage plans is delayed by the perversity of the nurse and we become anxious with Juliet at this unnecessary delay and relieved with Juliet when the message is given:

> *"Hie to high fortune! Honest nurse, farewell."*

Characters

JULIET

Juliet is very much in love in this scene. Anxiously she awaits the news of the plans for her wedding. She shows the tenderness and innocence of her love:

> *"What says he of our marriage? what of that?"*

She wishes to know has Romeo kept his promises as she has:

> *"Hie to high fortune!"*

Juliet is firm and determined in her dealings with the nurse. The nurse teases and tests her until she is almost angry:

> *"Are you so hot?"*

Yet Juliet is patient and sympathetic with the inconsiderate nurse!

> *"I'faith, I am sorry that thou art not well."*

*Now is the sun upon the highmost hill
Of this day's journey, and from nine till twelve
Is three long hours, yet she is not come.*   (Juliet, Act 2, Scene V)

THE NURSE

As before, the nurse shows her coarseness and self-importance. She teases Juliet for her own enjoyment, showing little consideration for Juliet's anxiety after waiting three hours for news:

> *"I am aweary, give me leave awhile:
> Fie, how my bones ache!"*

She is a contrast of Juliet, not only in her slowness but in her view of love. Juliet's love is tender and innocent, while the nurse enjoys thinking of the wedding night:

> *"To fetch a ladder, by the which your love
> Must climb a bird's nest soon when it is dark;
> I am the drudge and toil in your delight,"*

Scene VI

The Same. Friar Laurence's Cell
Enter Friar Laurence and Romeo

Friar Laurence

So smile the heaven upon this holy act,
That after hours with sorrow chide us not!

Romeo

Amen, amen! but come what sorrow can,
It cannot countervail[1] the exchange of joy
That one short minute gives me in her sight:
Do thou but close our hands with holy words,
Then love-devouring death do what he dare;
It is enough I may but call her mine.

[handwritten: Friar Surprised at romeos celebration of unending love]

Friar Laurence

These violent delights have violent ends,
And in their triumph die, like fire and powder,
Which, as they kiss consume: the sweetest honey
Is loathsome[2] in his own deliciousness
And in the taste confounds[3] the appetite:
Therefore love moderately; long love doth so;
Too swift[4] arrives as tardy as too slow.

[handwritten: Advises moderation and warns of the consequences]

Enter Juliet

Here comes the lady: O! so light a foot
Will ne'er wear out the everlasting flint:
A lover may bestride the gossamer[5]
That idles in the wanton[6] summer air,
And yet not fall; so light is vanity.

20

Juliet

Good even to my ghostly confessor.

Friar Laurence

Romeo shall thank thee, daughter, for us both.

Juliet

As much to him, else are his thanks too much.

Romeo

Ah! Juliet, if the measure of thy joy
Be heap'd like mine, and that thy skill be more
To blazon[7] it, then sweeten with thy breath
This neighbour air, and let rich music's tongue[8]
Unfold the imagin'd happiness[9] that both
Receive in either by this dear encounter.

[1] equal, outweigh

[2] so sweet that it is sickly

[3] destroys

[4] The more hurry, the less speed

[5] walk along a spider's web
[6] playful

[7] display

[8] sweet words (of love)
[9] inner happiness

Juliet

Conceit,[10] more rich in matter than in words,   30

Brags of his substance, not of ornament:

They are but beggars that can count their worth;

But my true love is grown to such excess

I cannot sum up sum of half my wealth.

Friar Laurence

Come, come with me, and we will make short work;

For, by your leaves, you shall not stay alone

Till holy church incorporate two in one.   *[Exeunt*

[10]true love does not need to express itself in a display of words

Summary – Time: Later on Monday afternoon

The Wedding

Friar Laurence and Romeo are waiting for Juliet in Friar Laurence's cell. The friar anxiously prays that God will bless the marriage and give no cause for regrets later on. Romeo asserts that their love will overcome all sorrows, even death itself, but the friar urges moderation in love in order to avoid tragedy.

Juliet arrives, and Romeo, full of emotion, declares how happy he is in love. Juliet says that her love is so wonderful that words cannot describe it. The friar declares that he must marry them at once and they go to be married quietly.

Scene Analysis

Love and Tragedy

The friar is surprised at Romeo's declaration of unending love which will defy even death:

> *"Do thou but close our hands with holy words,*
> *Then love-devouring death do what he dare;*
> *It is enough I may but call her mine."*

He advises moderation and warns of the consequences of excess:

> *"These violent delights have violent ends,*
> *And in their triumph die, like fire and powder,*
> *Which, as they kiss consume:"*

We are warned here that tragedy is about to follow this scene of love in the violence of the next scene.

But my true love is grown to such excess
I cannot sum up sum of half my wealth.

(Juliet, Act 2 Scene VI)

Love and Marriage

The lovers have already given themselves to each other in the "Balcony Scene". This scene brings that commitment to a formal conclusion in a quiet marriage. It is a scene of unbounded joy, despite its quietness. The lovers declare their youthful and mutual love, each in his and her own individual manner. Romeo is emotional and imaginative:

> *"Ah! Juliet, if the measure of thy joy*
> *Be heap'd like mine...*
> *...then sweeten with thy breath*
> *This neighbour air, and let rich music's tongue*
> *Unfold the imagin'd happiness that both*
> *Receive in either by this dear encounter."*

Juliet is practical but no less loving:

> *"I cannot sum up half my sum of wealth."*

This scene then is an idyllic calm before the storm.

Characters

Contrasting Characters

The friar is anxious but balanced in his view of love and marriage. He sees that excess of love, love that is too intense, cannot last. He is a force of coolness in the heat of the lovers' passions. Romeo is youthful, even naive, in his desire to defy the natural conditions of life through absolute love. He casts aside the tragic implications of the marriage:

> *"Amen, amen! but come what sorrow can,*
> *It cannot countervail the exchange of joy*
> *That one short minute gives me in her sight:"*

Juliet realises that love needs *"substance"* and must be more than words can express. She is passionately in love with Romeo but has her feet planted on the ground:

> *"Conceit, more rich in matter than in words,*
> *Brags of his substance, not of ornament:"*

Act 3
Scene I

Comedy
↓
Tragedy

Verona. A Public Place
Enter Mercutio, Benvolio, Page, and Servants

Benvolio

I pray thee, good Mercutio, let's retire:
The day is hot, the Capulets abroad,
And, if we meet, we shall not 'scape a brawl;
For now, these hot days, is the mad blood stirring.

Mercutio

Thou art like one of those fellows that when he
enters the confines of a tavern claps me his sword
upon the table and says, 'God send me no need of
thee!' and by the operation of the second cup[1]
draws him on the drawer,[2] when, indeed, there
is no need.   10

Benvolio

Am I like such a fellow?

Mercutio

Come, come, thou art as hot a Jack in thy mood as
any in Italy; and as soon moved to be moody, and
as soon moody to be moved.

Benvolio

And what to?

Mercutio

Nay, an there were two such, we should have none
shortly, for one would kill the other. Thou! why,
thou wilt quarrel with a man that hath a hair more or
a hair less in his beard than thou hast. Thou wilt
quarrel with a man for cracking nuts, having no   20
other reason but because thou hast hazel eyes.
What eye, but such an eye, would spy out such a
quarrel? Thy head is as full of quarrels as an egg is
full of meat, and yet thy head hath been beaten as
addle as an egg for quarrelling. Thou hast
quarrelled with a man for coughing in the street,
because he hath wakened thy dog that hath lain
asleep in the sun. Didst thou not fall out with a tailor
for wearing his new doublet before Easter? with
another, for tying his new shoes with old riband?   30
and yet thou wilt tutor me from[3] quarrelling!

[1] the effect of a second drink

[2] waiter

[3] teach me not to

Benvolio

An I were so apt to quarrel as thou art, any man
should buy the fee-simple of my life for an hour and
a quarter.

Mercutio

The fee-simple![4] O simple!

⁴full possession

Enter Tybalt, and Others

Benvolio

By my head, here come the Capulets.

Mercutio

By my heel, I care not.

Tybalt

Follow me close, for I will speak to them.
Gentlemen, good den! a word with one of you.

Mercutio

And but one word with one of us? Couple it with
omething; make it a word and a blow.

40

Tybalt

You shall find me apt enough to that, sir, an you will
give me occasion.

Mercutio

Could you not take some occasion without giving?

Tybalt

Mercutio, thou consort'st[5] with Romeo, —

⁵keep company with

Mercutio

Consort! What! dost thou make us minstrels? an
thou make minstrels of us, look to hear nothing but
discords: here's my fiddle-stick;[6] here's that
shall make you dance. 'Zounds![7] consort!

⁶rapier, sword
⁷By God's wounds!

Benvolio

We talk here in the public haunt of men:
Either withdraw unto some private place,
Or reason coldly of your grievances,
Or else depart; here all eyes gaze on us.

50

refuse to leave public streets

Mercutio

Men's eyes were made to look, and let them gaze;
I will not budge for no man's pleasure, I.

Enter Romeo

Tybalt
Well, peace be with you, sir. Here comes my man.

Mercutio
But I'll be hang'd, sir, if he wear your livery:[8]
Marry, go before to field, he'll be your follower;
Your worship in that sense may call him 'man.'

Tybalt
Romeo, the love I bear thee can afford   *challenging romeo to fight*   60
No better term than this, — thou art a villain.

Romeo
Tybalt, the reason that I have to love thee   *Trying to keep the peace*
Doth much excuse the appertaining[9] rage
To such a greeting; villain am I none,
Therefore farewell; I see thou know'st me not.

Tybalt
Boy, this shall not excuse the injuries   *Tybalt refuses to be appeased*
That thou hast done me; therefore turn and draw.

Romeo
I do protest I never injur'd thee,
But love thee better than thou canst devise,[10]
Till thou shalt know the reason of my love: 70
And so, good Capulet, which name I tender
As dearly as my own, be satisfied.

Mercutio
O calm, dishonourable, vile submission!   *mercutio fights Tybalt*
Alla stoccata[11] carries it away.   [Draws
Tybalt, you rat-catcher, will you walk?   *challenge to fight*

Tybalt
What wouldst thou have with me?

Mercutio
Good king of cats, nothing but one of your nine
lives, that I mean to make bold withal, and, as you
shall use[12] me hereafter, dry-beat[13] the rest of
the eight. Will you pluck your sword out of his   80
pilcher[14] by the ears? make haste, lest mine be
about your ears ere it be out.

Tybalt [Drawing]
I am for you.

Romeo
Gentle Mercutio, put thy rapier up.

use mercutio not to fight

Margin notes:
- [8] servant's uniform
- [9] accompanying
- [10] imagine
- [11] the first thrust
- [12] treat
- [13] thrash
- [14] scabbard

Mercutio

Come, sir, your passado.[15]   *[They fight*   [15]thrust

Romeo

Draw, Benvolio; beat down their weapons.
Gentlemen, for shame, forbear this outrage!
Tybalt, Mercutio, the prince expressly hath
Forbidden bandying[16] in Verona streets.   [16]brawling
Hold Tybalt! good Mercutio!   *90*

[Exeunt Tybalt and his Partisans

Mercutio

I am hurt?
A plague o' both your houses! I am sped.[17]   [17]wounded, slain
Is he gone, and hath nothing?

Benvolio

What! art thou hurt?   *Tries to downplay extent of the injury*

Mercutio

Ay, ay, a scratch, a scratch; marry, 'tis enough.
Where is my page? Go, villain, fetch a surgeon.

[Exit Page

Romeo

Courage, man; the hurt cannot be much.

Mercutio

No, 'tis not so deep as a well, nor so wide as a   *Play on words*
church door; but 'tis enough, 'twill serve: ask for   *Pun on grave*
me to-morrow, and you shall find me a grave man.   *100*
I am peppered,[18] I warrant, for this world. A   [18]killed
plague o' both your houses! 'Zounds, a dog, a rat,
a mouse, a cat, to scratch a man to death! a braggart,
a rogue, a villain, that fights by the book of
arithmetic! Why the devil came you between us? I
was hurt under your arm.   *Blaming romeo*

Romeo

I thought all for the best.

Mercutio

Help me into some house, Benvolio,
Or I shall faint. A plague o' both your houses!
They have made worms' meat of me: I have it,   *110*
And soundly too: — your houses!

[Exeunt Mercutio and Benvolio

Romeo
This gentleman, the prince's near ally,
My very friend, hath got his mortal hurt
In my behalf; my reputation stain'd
With Tybalt's slander, Tybalt, that an hour
Hath been my kinsman. O sweet Juliet!
Thy beauty hath made me effeminate,
And in my temper[19] soften'd valour's steel!

[19]character

Re-enter Benvolio

Benvolio
O Romeo, Romeo! brave Mercutio's dead;
That gallant spirit hath aspir'd[20] the clouds,   120
Which too untimely here did scorn the earth.

[20]climbed up to   *Mercutio dies*

Romeo
This day's black fate on more days doth depend;   *Domino effect*
This but begins the woe others must end.

Re-enter Tybalt

Benvolio
Here comes the furious Tybalt back again.
Romeo *—angry - ready to kill Tybalt*
Alive! in triumph! and Mercutio slain!
Away to heaven, respective lenity,[21]
And fire-ey'd fury be my conduct[22] now!
Now, Tybalt, take the villain back again
That late thou gav'st me; for Mercutio's soul
Is but a little way above our heads,   130
Staying for thine to keep him company:
Either thou, or I, or both, must go with him.

[21]mildness
[22]guide

Tybalt
Thou wretched boy, that didst consort him here,
Shalt with him hence.
Romeo
                    This shall determine that.
                        [They fight; Tybalt falls

Romeo kills Tybalt

Benvolio
Romeo, away! be gone!
The citizens are up, and Tybalt slain.
Stand not amaz'd: the prince will doom thee death
If thou art taken: hence! be gone! away!

Romeo

O! I am Fortune's fool.

Benvolio

               Why dost thou stay?   *140*

                            [Exit Romeo

               Enter Citizens, &c.

First Citizen

Which way ran he that kill'd Mercutio?
Tybalt, that murderer, which way ran he?

Benvolio

There lies that Tybalt.

First Citizen

             Up, sir, go with me.
I charge thee in the prince's name, obey.

       Enter Prince, attended; Montague, Capulet,
            their Wives, and Others

Prince

Where are the vile beginners of this fray?

Benvolio

O noble prince! I can discover[23] all   [23]reveal
The unlucky manage[24] of this fatal brawl: [24]course
There lies the man, slain by young Romeo,
That slew thy kinsman, brave Mercutio.

Lady Capulet

Tybalt, my cousin! O my brother's child!   *150*
O prince! O husband! O! the blood is spill'd
Of my dear kinsman. Prince, as thou art true,
For blood of ours shed blood of Montague.
O cousin, cousin!

Prince

Benvolio, who began this bloody fray?

Benvolio

Tybalt, here slain, whom Romeo's hand did slay:
Romeo, that spoke him fair, bade him bethink
How nice[25] the quarrel was, and urg'd withal   [25]trivial
Your high displeasure: all this, uttered
With gentle breath, calm look, knees humbly
      bow'd,   *160*
Could not take truce with the unruly spleen[26]   [26]bad temper
Of Tybalt deaf to peace, but that he tilts
With piercing steel at bold Mercutio's breast,
Who, all as hot, turns deadly point to point,

And, with a martial scorn, with one hand beats
Cold death aside, and with the other sends
It back to Tybalt, whose dexterity

27returns

Retorts[27] it: Romeo he cries aloud,
'Hold, friends! friends, part!' and, swifter than his
          tongue,
His agile arm beats down their fatal points,   170
And 'twixt them rushes; underneath whose arm

28hostile

An envious[28] thrust from Tybalt hit the life
Of stout Mercutio, and then Tybalt fled;
But by and by comes back to Romeo,
Who had but newly entertain'd revenge,
And to 't they go like lighting, for, ere I
Could draw to part them, was stout Tybalt slain,
And, as he fell, did Romeo turn and fly.
This is the truth, or let Benvolio die.

Lady Capulet

He is a kinsman to the Montague;   180
Affection makes him false, he speaks not true:
Some twenty of them fought in this black strife
And all those twenty could but kill one life.
I beg for justice, which thou, prince, must give;
Romeo slew Tybalt, Romeo must not live.

Prince

Romeo slew him, he slew Mercutio;
Who now the price of his dear blood doth owe?

Montague

Not Romeo, prince, he was Mercutio's friend,
His fault concludes but what the law should end,
The life of Tybalt.

Prince

                    And for that offence   190
Immediately we do exile him hence:
I have an interest in your hate's proceeding,
My blood for your rude brawls doth lie a-bleeding;

29fine, punish

But I'll amerce[29] you with so strong a fine
That you shall all repent the loss of mine.
I will be deaf to pleading and excuses;
Nor tears nor prayers shall purchase out abuses;
Therefore use none; let Romeo hence in haste,
Else, when he's found, that hour is his last.
Bear hence this body and attend our will: 200

30lenient punishment
   encourages crime

Mercy but murders,[30] pardoning those that kill.   [Exeunt

Prince has banished Romeo from Verona,
(if he is found in verona he will be executed)

Summary – Time: Monday afternoon soon after the marriage

The Climax of the Drama

Mercutio and Benvolio, on the streets in Verona, talk of the danger of a brawl, since the Capulets are on the streets and the hot weather may make tempers flare. Benvolio, the peace-maker, advises that they leave since Mercutio may cause trouble.

Tybalt comes on the scene, looking for Romeo, and Mercutio deliberately insults him and draws his sword. Benvolio tries to calm them down.

Romeo enters the scene and Tybalt tries to provoke him to fight. Romeo is unwilling since Tybalt is now his new cousin. Tybalt insults Romeo, calling him *"boy"*. Mercutio is ashamed of Romeo's cowardice, as he sees it, and draws his sword. As Romeo tries to come between them, Mercutio is mortally wounded by Tybalt who tries to escape.

Mercutio curses both houses of Verona, Tybalt himself and Romeo, who indirectly caused his death by getting in the way. Benvolio then helps him into some house and Romeo is left on his own as Mercutio dies.

Romeo sees the disgrace he has caused and when Tybalt returns, Romeo seeks to avenge his friend's death. Tybalt taunts Romeo and they fight. Tybalt is killed and Romeo flees, remembering the Prince's decree of death.

The Prince arrives and the Capulets demand the life of Romeo for killing Tybalt. Benvolio tries to explain what really happened and the Prince makes his decision. Since Tybalt murdered Mercutio, the punishment for Romeo is exile and both houses are to be fined heavily. Romeo must leave Verona on pain of death.

Scene Analysis

The Climax of the Tragedy

This scene is the turning-point of the drama. Up to now, the love relationship of Romeo and Juliet ran smoothly with few real obstacles. Now Romeo is banished on the very day of his wedding and the marriage seems doomed. It is a formidable obstacle:

> *"This day's black fate on more days doth depend;*
> *This but begins the woe others must end."*

and:

> *"O! I am Fortune's fool."*

The hate and rivalries of Verona begin to close in on Romeo's new love.

This scene is the turning point of Romeo's life. He is caught in a trap of Fate. He tries to heal the wounds of the feud, believing that love can overcome hate.

> *"I do protest, I never injur'd thee,*
> *But love thee better than thou canst devise,"*

Will you pluck your sword out of his
pilcher by the ears? make haste, lest mine be
about your ears ere it be out.

(Mercutio, Act 3, Scene I)

He reacts honourably to his friend's death in challenging Tybalt and thereby puts himself and his love at risk. His choice was noble but he must now suffer tragically for it. Such is the extent of hate in Verona that even an honourable deed will bring fateful consequences.

> *"I thought all for the best."*

Thus this scene presents us with the keynote to the tragedy and the events proceed more swiftly towards tragedy after this scene.

The climax is established skilfully and gradually in this scene:

1. Violence threatens, we learn from Mercutio and Benvolio's conversation.
2. Tybalt provokes Mercutio and then Romeo, who desires peace.
3. Mercutio, thinking Romeo a coward, defends their honour against Tybalt, who kills him.
4. Romeo avenges Mercutio's death and flees.
5. The prince exiles Romeo on pain of death, having heard Benvolio's account of the fight.

Characters

ROMEO

Romeo is transformed by his love for Juliet. He greets Tybalt as a friend:

> *"Tybalt, the reason that I have to love thee*
> *Doth much excuse the appertaining rage*
> *To such a greeting: villain am I none,"*

He tries to appease Tybalt who is insulting him and demands a fight. He tries to separate Mercutio and Tybalt by coming between them:

> *"...Romeo he cries aloud,*
> *'Hold friends! friends, part!'*
> *and, swifter than his tongue,*
> *His agile arm beats down their fatal points,*
> *And 'twixt them rushes;..."*

Romeo has learned moral courage.

Romeo is still rash and impetuous, despite his nobility. When Mercutio, his friend, is killed, Romeo loses control and becomes angry. He abandons all caution for *"fire-ey'd fury"*. Under the stress of the moment, he has made himself, *"Fortune's fool"* and disaster follows.

MERCUTIO

In this scene Mercutio is quarrelsome and on the lookout for adventure. He provokes Tybalt as soon as he sees him:

> *"...make it a word and a blow."*

He is courageous and loves a challenge. He cannot abide how Romeo seems to be a coward:

> *"O calm, dishonourable, vile submission!"*

His fearlessness leads to his own death and Romeo's banishment.

He is as always a realist and a wit, disliking false show or hypocrisy. Even when he is dying he has time to joke:

> *...ask for me to-morrow, and you shall find me a grave man."*

He contrasts with Romeo's idealism.

BENVOLIO

Benvolio is a lover of peace and has little interest in sword fights. He tries to separate Mercutio from Tybalt when they fight. He realises earlier that they would be more sensible to stay off the streets to *"'scape a brawl"*.

Benvolio is honest and trustworthy. He gives a fair account of the slayings to the Prince and it is to him that the dying Mercutio turns for help. He is loyal to his friends and the house of Montague.

TYBALT

Tybalt is "an angry young man" who broods on revenge for past insults and provokes others to fight him:

> *"Romeo, the hate I bear thee can afford*
> *No better term than this, — thou art a villain."*

Yet Tybalt has a sense of honour, but is proud and boastful too. It is he who tries to provoke Romeo, but Mercutio is the one who started the insults. He is only partially to blame.

> *"Thou, wretched boy, that did'st consort him here,*
> *Shalt with him hence."*

PRINCE ESCALUS

The Prince represents law and order in Verona. His justice is tempered with mercy. His verdict on Romeo is fair since Romeo had some justification for killing Tybalt:

> *"His fault concludes but what the law should end,*
> *The life of Tybalt."*

But mercy begets murder:

> *"Mercy but murders, pardoning those that kill."*

So Romeo must be exiled.

LADY CAPULET

Lady Capulet is fierce in nature and demands blood for blood. She has no mercy for Romeo. She has no thought of peace, only of revenge.

> *"Romeo slew Tybalt, Romeo must not live."*

Scene II

The Same. Capulet's Orchard. Enter Juliet

Juliet

Gallop apace, you fiery-footed steeds,[1]   [1]horses of the sun-god
Towards Phoebus' lodging;[2] such a waggoner   [2]the sun
As Phaethon[3] would whip you to the west,   [3]son of Phoebus (Apollo)
And bring in cloudy night immediately.
Spread thy close curtain, love-performing night!
That runaway's[4] eyes may wink, and Romeo   [4]wanderers
Leap to these arms, untalk'd of and unseen!
Lovers can see to do their amorous rites
By their own beauties; or, if love be blind,
It best agrees with night. Come, civil night,   10
Thou sober-suited matron, all in black,
And learn me how to lose a winning match,
Play'd for a pair of stainless maidenhoods:
Hood my unmann'd blood, bating in my cheeks,
With thy black mantle; till strange love, grown bold,
Think true love acted simple modesty.
Come, night! come, Romeo! come, thou day in
      night!
For thou wilt lie upon the wings of night,
Whiter than new snow on a raven's back.
Come, gentle night; come, loving, black-brow'd
      night,   20
Give me my Romeo: and, when I shall die,
Take him and cut him out in little stars,
And he will make the face of heaven so fine
That all the world will be in love with night,
And pay no worship to the garish[5] sun.   [5]bright
O! I have bought the mansion of a love,
But not possess'd it, and, though I am sold,
Not yet enjoy'd. So tedious is this day
As is the night before some festival
To an impatient child that hath new robes   30
And may not wear them. O! here comes my nurse,

Enter Nurse with cords

And she brings news; and every tongue that
      speaks
But Romeo's name speaks heavenly eloquence.
Now nurse, what news? What hast thou there? the
      cords
That Romeo bade thee fetch?

Nurse

        Ay, ay, the cords.

                        [Throws them down

Juliet

Ah me! What news? why dost thou wring thy
      hands?

Nurse

Ah well-a-day! he's dead, he's dead, he's dead!
We are undone, lady, we are undone!
Alack the day! he's gone, he's killed, he's dead!

Juliet

Can heaven be so envious?

Nurse

             Romeo can,   *40*
Though heaven cannot. O! Romeo, Romeo;
Who ever would have thought it? Romeo!

Juliet

What devil art thou that dost torment me thus?
This torture should be roar'd in dismal hell.
Hath Romeo slain himself! say thou but 'I,'
And that bare vowel, 'I,' shall poison more
Than the death-darting eye of cockatrice:[6]
I am not I, if there be such an 'I;'
Or those eyes shut that make thee answer 'I.'
If he be slain, say 'I;' or if not 'no:'   *50*
Brief sounds determine of my weal[7] or woe.

Nurse

I saw the wound, I saw it with mine eyes,
God save the mark! here on his manly breast:
A piteous corse, a bloody piteous corse;[8]
Pale, pale as ashes, all bedaub'd in blood,
All in gore blood; I swounded at the sight.

Juliet

O break, my heart! — poor bankrupt, break at
      once!
To prison, eyes, ne'er look on liberty!
Vile earth, to earth resign;[9] end motion here;
And thou and Romeo press one heavy bier!   *60*

Nurse

O Tybalt, Tybalt! the best friend I had:
O courteous Tybalt! honest gentleman!
That ever I should live to see thee dead!

[6] a serpent with a killing look

[7] welfare

[8] corpse

[9] body return to dust

Juliet

What storm is this that blows so contrary?[10]
Is Romeo slaughter'd, and is Tybalt dead?
My dearest cousin, and my dearer lord?
Then, dreadful trumpet, sound the general doom![11]
For who is living if those two are gone?

[10]in different directions

[11]the day of judgment

Nurse

Tybalt is gone, and Romeo banished;
Romeo, that kill'd him, he is banished.   *70*

Juliet

O God! did Romeo's hand shed Tybalt's blood?

Nurse

It did, it did; alas the day! it did.

Juliet

O serpent heart, hid with a flowering face!
Did ever dragon keep so fair a cave?
Beautiful tyrant! fiend angelical!
Dove-feather'd raven! wolvish-ravening lamb!
Despised substance of divinest show!
Just opposite to what thou justly seem'st;
A damned saint, an honourable villain!
O, nature! what hadst thou to do in hell   *80*
When thou didst bower[12] the spirit of a fiend
In mortal paradise of such sweet flesh?
Was ever book containing such vile matter
So fairly bound? O! that deceit should dwell
In such a gorgeous palace.

[12]enclose

Nurse

                         There's no trust,
No faith, no honesty in men: all naught,
All perjur'd, all dissemblers,[13] all forsworn.
Ah! where's my man? give me some *aqua vitae*
These griefs, these woes, these sorrows make me
       old.
Shame come to Romeo!

[13]deceivers

Juliet

                         Blister'd be thy tongue   *90*
For such a wish! he was not born to shame:
Upon his brow shame is asham'd to sit;
For 'tis a throne where honour may be crown'd
Sole monarch of the universal earth.
O! what a beast was I to chide at him.

Nurse

Will you speak well of him that kill'd your cousin?

Juliet

Shall I speak ill of him that is my husband?

Ah! poor my lord, what tongue shall smooth [14] thy
    name,

When I, thy three-hours wife, have mangled it?

But, wherefore, villain, didst thou kill my cousin?   100

That villain cousin would have kill'd my husband:

Back, foolish tears, back to your native spring;

Your tributary drops belong to woe,

Which you, mistaking, offer up to joy. [15]

My husband lives, that Tybalt would have slain;

And Tybalt's dead, that would have slain my
    husband:

All this is comfort; wherefore weep I then?

Some word there was, worser than Tybalt's death,

That murder'd me: I would forget it fain; [16]

But O! it presses to my memory,   110

Like damned guilty deeds to sinners' minds.

'Tybalt is dead, and Romeo banished!'

That 'banished,' that one word 'banished,'

Hath slain ten thousand Tybalts. Tybalt's death

Was woe enough, if it had ended there:

Or, if sour woe delights in fellowship,

And needly will be rank'd with other griefs,

Why follow'd not, when she said 'Tybalt's dead',

Thy father, or thy mother, nay, or both,

Which modern [17] lamentation might have mov'd?   120

But with a rearward [18] following Tybalt's death,

'Romeo is banished!' to speak that word

Is father, mother, Tybalt, Romeo, Juliet,

All slain, all dead: 'Romeo is banished!'

There is no end, no limit, measure, bound

In that word's death; no words can that woe
    sound. —

Where is my father and my mother, nurse?

Nurse

Weeping and wailing over Tybalt's corse:

Will you go to them? I will bring you thither.

Juliet

Wash they his wounds with tears: mine shall be
    spent,   130

When theirs are dry, for Romeo's banishment.

Take up those cords. Poor ropes, you are beguil'd,

[14] speak well of

[15] attribute to joy

[16] gladly

[17] ordinary
[18] further incident

Both you and I, for Romeo is exil'd:
He made you for a highway to my bed,
But I, a maid, die maiden-widowed.
Come, cords; come, nurse; I'll to my wedding bed;
And death, not Romeo, take my maidenhead!

Nurse
Hie to your chamber; I'll find Romeo
To comfort you: I wot[19] well where he is.   [19]know
Hark ye, your Romeo will be here to-night: 140
I'll to him; he is hid at Laurence' cell.

Juliet
O! find him; give this ring to my true knight,
And bid him come to take his last farewell.   [Exeunt

Summary – Time: Monday afternoon, three hours after the marriage

Juliet Awaits her Husband

As Juliet waits impatiently for the wedding night, full of joy and anticipation and blissfully unaware of the violent events that have happened, she speaks her wedding song. She bids the night to fall quickly and bring her husband to her loving arms.

Suddenly the nurse enters in confusion, shocked at the news she has just heard. She gives Juliet the impression that Romeo is dead and Juliet feels betrayed and full of despair. Then the nurse speaks clearly and tells Juliet of Tybalt's death and Romeo's banishment, and Juliet is full of grief for Romeo.

Juliet recovers her composure when the nurse begins to abuse Romeo for his actions. Juliet sees that her first loyalty must be to her husband before her family.

Finally Juliet begins to understand her situation. The banishment of Romeo is like his death and she will be a widow before she becomes a wife. As the nurse goes to bring Romeo to Juliet, Juliet realises that this will be a last farewell before death.

Scene Analysis

Juliet as an Eager Bride

Juliet impatiently looks forward to her wedding night, eager to consummate the marriage. In her wedding song, she shows her deepest feelings of love:

"Spread thy close curtain, love-performing night!
That runaway's eyes may wink, and Romeo
Leap to these arms, untalk'd of and unseen!...
Come, night! come, Romeo! come, thou day in night!"

Like a child, she looks forward to a night of blissful happiness:

> *"...that hath new robes/And may not wear them."*

Juliet Copes with Tragic News

Juliet's happiness comes to an abrupt end when the shocked nurse brings sad news of Romeo's banishment. Juliet is confused and grief-stricken at first:

> *"O break, my heart! — poor bankrupt, break at once!"*

Then she feels her husband has betrayed her:

> *"O serpent heart, hid with a flowering face!...*
> *Beautiful tyrant! fiend angelical!"*

At last she realises Romeo was not to blame and did not let her down:

> *"O! what a beast was I to chide at him."*

Finally she sees that their love is doomed before it can be fulfilled:

> *"But I, a maid, die maiden-widowed."*

She courageously arranges for her husband to *"come to take his last farewell"*. She copes with the tragic news in a mature and dignified manner, preferring death to separation.

Characters

JULIET

Juliet shows heroic courage and a new maturity in the way she deals with the stress of Romeo's banishment. She confronts the sad news bravely, thinks it out and comes to terms with it:

> *"Back, foolish tears, back to your native spring;*
> *Your tributary drops belong to woe,*
> *Which you, mistaking, offer up to joy.*
> *My husband lives, that Tybalt would have slain;"*

She is able to count her blessings with a realism greater than Romeo could manage.

The depth and range of her emotions transform her into a heroic figure, as befits her tragic role. Her feelings range from ecstatic happiness to extreme despair, from anger and sadness to optimism and calmness and even from hate to love. She wins our admiration.

THE NURSE

Yet again the nurse keeps Juliet in suspense, but this time it is the real shock of the tragic news and not a desire to tease that is the reason. In the end, the nurse shows sympathy for Juliet, separated from her husband, and offers to bring Romeo to console her. The nurse, by her seemingly insensitive comments and questions, also helps Juliet to come to terms with her conflicting emotions concerning Romeo.

Scene III

The Same. Friar Laurence's Cell
Enter Friar Laurence

Friar Laurence
Romeo, come forth; come forth, thou fearful man:
Affliction is enamour'd of thy parts
And thou art wedded to calamity.

Enter Romeo

Romeo
Father, what news? what is the prince's doom?[1]
What sorrow craves acquaintance[2] at my hand,
That I yet know not?

                   [1]sentence

                   [2]awaits me

Friar Laurence
              Too familiar
Is my dear son with such sour company:
I bring thee tidings of the prince's doom.

Romeo
What less than doomsday[3] is the prince's doom?

                   [3]death

Friar Laurence
A gentler judgment vanish'd from his lips   *10*
Not body's death, but body's banishment.

Romeo
Ha! banishment! be merciful, say 'death;'
For exile hath more terror in his look,
Much more than death: do not say 'banishment.'

Friar Laurence
Hence from Verona art thou banished.
Be patient, for the world is broad and wide.

Romeo
There is no world without Verona walls,
But purgatory, torture, hell itself.
Hence banished is banish'd from the world,
And world's exile is death; then 'banished,'   *20*
Is death mis-term'd. Calling death 'banished.'
Thou cutt'st my head off with a golden axe,
And smil'st upon the stroke that murders me.

Friar Laurence
O deadly sin! O rude unthankfulness!
Thy fault our law calls death; but the kind prince,

Taking thy part, hath rush'd aside the law,
And turn'd that black word death to banishment:
This is dear mercy, and thou seest it not.

Romeo

'Tis torture, and not mercy: heaven is here,
Where Juliet lives; and every cat and dog   30
And little mouse, every unworthy thing,
Live here in heaven and may look on her;
But Romeo may not: more validity,⁴
More honourable state, more courtship lives
In carrion flies than Romeo: they may seize
On the white wonder of dear Juliet's hand,
And steal immortal blessings from her lips,
Who, even in pure and vestal⁵ modesty,
Still blush, as thinking their own kisses sin;
Flies may do this, but I from this must fly: 40
They are free men, but I am banished.
And sayest thou yet that exile is not death?
Hadst thou no poison mix'd, no sharp-ground
    knife,
No sudden mean of death,⁶ though ne'er so mean,
But 'banished' to kill me? 'Banished!'
O friar! the damned use that word in hell;
Howlings attend it: how hast thou the heart,
Being a divine, a ghostly confessor,
A sin-absolver, and my friend profess'd,
To mangle me with that word 'banished?'   50

Friar Laurence

Thou fond⁷ mad man, hear me a little speak.

Romeo

O! thou wilt speak again of banishment.

Friar Laurence

I'll give thee armour to keep off that word;
Adversity's sweet milk,⁸ philosophy,
To comfort thee, though thou art banished.

Romeo

Yet 'banished!' Hang up philosophy!
Unless philosophy can make a Juliet,
Displant a town, reverse a prince's doom,
It helps not, it prevails not: talk no more.

Friar Laurence

O! then I see that madmen have no ears,   60

⁴value
⁵virgin
⁶method of death
⁷foolish
⁸remedy

once again Juliet is compared to being heaven like.
Romeo's wallowing in self pity

(Laurence saying that romeo refuses to listen to reason

Romeo
How should they, when that wise men have no
          eyes?

Friar Laurence
Let me dispute with thee of thy estate.[9]

[9]situation

Romeo
Thou canst not speak of that thou dost not feel:
Wert thou as young as I, Juliet thy love,
An hour but married, Tybalt murdered,
Doting like me, and like me banished,
Then mightst thou speak, then mightst thou tear
          thy hair,
And fall upon the ground, as I do now,
Taking the measure[10] of an unmade grave.

                              [Knocking within

[10]measuring you; stretching
    out

Friar Laurence
Arise; one knocks: good Romeo, hide thyself.   *70*

Romeo
Not I; unless the breath of heart-sick groans,
Mist-like, infold me from the search of eyes.

                              [Knocking

Friar Laurence
Hark! how they knock. Who's there? Romeo
          arise;
Thou wilt be taken. Stay awhile! Stand up;

                              [Knocking

Run to my study. By and by! God's will!
What simpleness is this! I come, I come!

                              [Knocking

Who knocks so hard? whence come you? what's
          your will?

Nurse *[Within]*
Let me come in, and you shall know my errand:
I come from Lady Juliet.

Friar Laurence
                    Welcome, then.

                    Enter Nurse

Nurse
O holy friar! O! tell me, holy friar,   *80*
Where is my lady's lord? where's Romeo?

Friar Laurence

There on the ground, with his own tears made
    drunk.

Nurse

O! he is even in my mistress' case,
Just in her case! O woeful sympathy!
Piteous predicament! Even so lies she,
Blubbering and weeping, weeping and blubbering.
Stand up, stand up; stand, an you be a man:
For Juliet's sake, for her sake, rise and stand;
Why should you fall into so deep an O?[11]

(handwritten margin note: Nurse urges romeo to be brave and mature and to the consequnc of his action for Juliets Sake)

(handwritten right margin: stand up & be a man)

Romeo

Nurse!   90

Nurse

Ah, sir! ah, sir! Well, death's the end of all.

Romeo

Spak'st thou of Juliet? how is it with her?
Doth she not think me an old murderer,
Now I have stain'd the childhood of our joy
With blood remov'd but little from her own?
Where is she? and how doth she? and what says
My conceal'd[12] lady to our cancell'd love?

Nurse

O! she says nothing, sir, but weeps and weeps;
And now falls on her bed; and then starts up,
And Tybalt calls, and then on Romeo cries,   100
And then falls down again.

Romeo

               As if that name,
Shot from the deadly level[13] of a gun,
Did murder her; as that name's cursed hand
Murder'd her kinsman. O! tell me, friar, tell me,
In what vile part of this anatomy
Doth my name lodge? tell me, that I may sack[14]
The hateful mansion.   [Drawing his sword

(handwritten right margin: not benevolent attempts to kill himself)

Friar Laurence

              Hold thy desperate hand:
Art thou a man? thy form cries out thou art:
Thy tears are womanish; thy wild acts denote
The unreasonable fury of a beast: 110
Unseemly woman in a seeming man;
And ill-beseeming beast in seeming both!

(handwritten margin note: Friar reasons with romeo with what action to take and prevents him from killing himself. He also helps him relise that he romeo didn't kill)

[11]despair
[12]frustrated
[13]aim
[14]plunder

Thou hast amaz'd me: by my holy order,
I thought thy disposition[15] better temper'd.[16]
Hast thou slain Tybalt? wilt thou slay thyself?
And slay thy lady that in thy life lives,
By doing damned hate upon thyself?
Why rail'st thou on thy birth, the heaven, and
        earth?
Since birth, and heaven, and earth, all three do
        meet
In thee at once, which thou at once wouldst lose.   120
Fie, fie! thou sham'st thy shape, thy love, thy wit,[17]
Which, like a usurer, abound'st in all,
And usest none in that true use indeed
Which should bedeck[18] thy shape, thy love, thy wit.
Thy noble shape is but a form of wax,
Digressing[19] from the valour of a man;
Thy dear love, sworn, but hollow perjury,
Killing that love which thou hast vow'd to cherish;
Thy wit, that ornament to shape and love,
Misshapen in the conduct[20] of them both,   130
Like powder in a skilless soldier's flask,
To set a-fire by thine own ignorance,
And thou dismember'd[21] with thine own defence.
What! rouse thee, man; thy Juliet is alive,
For whose dear sake thou wast but lately dead;
There art thou happy: Tybalt would kill thee,
But thou slew'st Tybalt; there art thou happy too:
The law that threaten'd death becomes thy friend,
And turns it to exile; there art thou happy:
A pack of blessings light upon thy back;   140
Happiness courts thee in her best array;
But, like a misbehav'd and sullen wench,
Thou pout'st upon thy fortune and thy love.
Take heed, take heed, for such die miserable.
Go, get thee to thy love, as was decreed,
Ascend her chamber, hence and comfort her;
But look thou stay not till the watch be set,
For then thou canst not pass to Mantua;
Where thou shalt live, till we can find a time
To blaze[22] your marriage, reconcile your friends,   150
Beg pardon of the prince, and call thee back
With twenty hundred thousand times more joy
Than thou went'st forth in lamentation.
Go before, nurse: commend me to thy lady;
And bid her hasten all the house to bed,

[15] character
[16] stronger
[17] intelligence
[18] decorate; honour
[19] deviating from
[20] management
[21] torn apart
[22] announce

[handwritten margin note:] Plan romeo is to spend his wedding night with his bride, he must leave before sunrise and must flee to Mantua. He is to remain there until the time is right for their marriage to be announced. When this is done it is expected that romeo is to be forgiven his misdeeds and should be allowed back into verona

Which heavy sorrow makes them apt unto:
Romeo is coming.

Nurse
O Lord! I could have stay'd here all the night
To hear good counsel: O! what learning is.
My Lord, I'll tell my lady you will come.   160

Romeo
Do so, and bid my sweet prepare to chide.

Nurse
Here, sir, a ring she bid me give you, sir.
Hie you, make haste, for it grows very late.

Romeo
How well my comfort is reviv'd by this!

Friar Laurence
Go hence; good-night; and here stands all your
    state.[23]
Either be gone before the watch be set,
Or by the break of day disguis'd from hence;
Sojourn[24] in Mantua; I'll find out your man,
And he shall signify from time to time
Every good hap[25] to you that chances here.   170
Give me thy hand; 'tis late: farewell; good-night.

Romeo
But that a joy past joy calls out on me,
It were a grief so brief to part with thee:
Farewell.

[Exeunt

[23]fortune

[24]stay

[25]fortune

Summary – Time: Late on Monday evening

Romeo in Dire Straits

Friar Laurence tells Romeo, who is hidden in the friar's cell, that he is to be exiled from Verona for killing Tybalt. Romeo is distraught at this news since banishment means separation from Juliet and as such is worse than death. The friar tries to comfort Romeo in his despair.

The nurse arrives and tells Romeo of Juliet's distress and is disgusted at Romeo's childish behaviour when Juliet needs him to be strong. Romeo is filled with guilt and tries to stab himself, but the friar prevents him. In a long lecture, the friar tries to help Romeo to be strong. Romeo has much to be thankful for and should count his blessings and go to Juliet as arranged. The friar promises to do his best to sort out the problems so that Romeo can return from exile in Mantua. Romeo agrees and leaves the friar who will keep in touch through Romeo's servant, Balthasar.

Scene Analysis

A Depressed Romeo

Under stress, Romeo, unlike Juliet in *Act 3 Scene II*, resorts to despair and attempts suicide. The nurse has to remind him to be strong for Juliet:

> *"Stand up, stand up; stand, an you be a man:*
> *For Juliet's sake, for her sake, rise and stand;"*

The friar reproves him for selfish despair:

> *"Thy tears are womanish; thy wild acts denote*
> *The unreasonable fury of a beast;*
> *Unseemly woman in a seeming man;"*

Romeo loses his self-control under stress, but his love for Juliet saves him:

> *"But that a joy past joy calls out on me,*
> *It were a grief, so brief to part with thee."*

Like Juliet, separation for Romeo is worse than death, but he begins to pull himself together when the nurse gives him Juliet's ring as a love-token:

> *"How well my comfort is revived by this!"*

The outlook is more hopeful.

A Note of Suspense

This scene keeps the audience in suspense waiting for Romeo to control himself and become more manly. The *"knocking within"* when the nurse arrives further intensifies this excitement as the friar and Romeo fear for Romeo's safety if he is found hiding:

> *"Romeo, arise;*
> *Thou wilt be taken."*

Further suspense is caused when the friar promises,

> *"To blaze your marriage, reconcile your friends,*
> *Beg pardon of the prince, and call thee back*
> *With twenty hundred thousand times more joy*
> *Than thou went'st forth in lamentation."*

However unlikely, we hope that the friar's good intentions will be realised and the lovers will be reunited.

But that a joy past joy calls out on me,
It were a grief so brief to part with thee:
Farewell.

(Romeo, Act 3, Scene III)

Characters

ROMEO

Romeo is childish in his reactions to grief and indulges in self-pity. The nurse is disgusted and tells him to be a man for Juliet who needs him:

> *"Stand up, stand up; stand an you be a man:*
> *For Juliet's sake, for her sake, rise and stand;"*

Romeo loses self-control and his guilt at his banishment plunges him into deep despair. He attempts suicide:

> *"What less than doomsday is the prince's doom?"*

Romeo is unable to come to terms with his deep despair. Unlike Juliet, he is unwilling or unable to count his blessings; his mind can focus on nothing except his loss:

> *"'Tis torture, and not mercy: heaven is here,*
> *Where Juliet lives; and every cat and dog*
> *And little mouse, every unworthy thing,*
> *Live here in heaven and may look on her;*
> *But Romeo may not:"*

Juliet then wins our sympathy and admiration in the parallel scene *(Act 3, Scene II)* but Romeo merely gains our sympathy in this scene. However, he revives on receiving Juliet's ring from the nurse:

> *"How well my comfort is reviv'd by this!"*

FRIAR LAURENCE

The friar is Romeo's father-confessor and friend, whom Romeo loves and respects. He helps Romeo by his kindness to regain his will to live and to see reason when Romeo is most in need of a calm adviser in his confused state of mind:

> *"Thy dear love, sworn, but hollow perjury,*
> *Killing that love which thou hast vow'd to cherish;"*

The friar's intentions are kind and charitable, but he is sometimes impractical. Romeo, in his grief, is in no fit state to take seriously a long philosophical sermon and but for the arrival of the nurse might not have pulled himself together. On receiving the ring Romeo says:

> *"How well my comfort is reviv'd by this!"*

The friar's zeal for peace and happiness far outweighs his ability to achieve them. He intends to solve Romeo's and Verona's problems so that Romeo may return:

> *"With twenty hundred thousand times more joy*
> *Than thou went'st forth in lamentation."*

He is nothing if not optimistic.

Scene IV

The Same. A Room in Capulet's House
Enter Capulet, Lady Capulet, and Paris

Capulet
Things have fall'n out,[1] sir, so unluckily,
That we have had no time to move our daughter:
Look you, she lov'd her kinsman Tybalt dearly,
And so did I: well, we were born to die.
'Tis very late, she'll not come down to-night:
I promise you, but for your company,
I would have been a-bed an hour ago.

Paris
These times of woe afford no times to woo.
Madam, good-night: commend me to your
        daughter.

Lady Capulet
I will, and know her mind early to-morrow;   *10*
To-night she's mew'd[2] up to her heaviness.

Capulet
Sir Paris, I will make a desperate tender[3]
Of my child's love: I think she will be rul'd
In all respects by me; nay, more, I doubt it not.
Wife go you to her ere you go to bed;
Acquaint her here of my son Paris' love;
And bid her, mark you me, on Wednesday next —
But, soft! what day is this?

Paris
                              Monday, my lord.

Capulet
Monday! ha, ha! Well, Wednesday is too soon;
O'Thursday let it be: o' Thursday, tell her,   *20*
She shall be married to this noble earl.
Will you be ready? do you like this haste?
We'll keep no great ado;[4] a friend or two;
For, hark you, Tybalt being slain so late,
It may be thought we held him carelessly,[5]
Being our kinsman, if we revel much.
Therefore we'll have some half a dozen friends,
And there an end. But what say you to Thursday?

[1] happened

[2] shut up

[3] risk a bold offer

[4] fuss

[5] without respect

Paris
My lord, I would that Thursday were to-morrow.

Capulet
Well, get you gone: o'Thursday be it then,　　　　　　　*30*
Go you to Juliet ere you go to bed,
Prepare her, wife, against[6] this wedding-day.　　　　　　[6]for
Farewell, my lord. Light to my chamber, ho!
Afore me![7] it is so very very late,　　　　　　　　　[7]Upon my word
That we may call it early by and by.
Good-night.

　　　　　　　　　　　　　　　　[Exeunt

Summary – Time: very early on Tuesday morning

Capulet Arranges a Marriage with Paris

In the early hours of Tuesday morning, Capulet explains to Paris that he has had no opportunity to consult Juliet about a marriage to Paris, due to the death of Tybalt. Lady Capulet promises to inform Paris the next day about Juliet's intentions.

As Paris is about to leave, Capulet decides that Juliet will marry Paris on Thursday, since he feels sure that his daughter will obey her father's wishes in this matter. Lady Capulet is to inform Juliet of his decision. Paris promises to be ready on Thursday and leaves Capulet's mansion.

Scene Analysis

A New Turn of Events

Ironically, just as Romeo and Juliet enjoy their wedding night, events outside their control begin to happen. Her father, not knowing that Juliet is already married, promises Paris that Juliet will marry him on Thursday, only three days away. Unintentionally, her loving father places Juliet in an extremely difficult situation to add to her already insurmountable problems. Swiftly the impending tragedy moves closer:

> *"Sir Paris, I will make a desperate tender*
> *Of my child's love: I think she will be rul'd*
> *In all respects by me; nay, more, I doubt it not."*

These times of woe afford no times to woo.
Madam, good-night: commend me to your
daughter.   *(Paris, Act 3, Scene IV)*

Characters

CAPULET

Capulet is a conventional father in his attitude to his daughter and to marriage. He expects his daughter to obey his will and marry Paris. Social esteem, which his family will gain from marrying the Prince's kinsman, takes precedence over love for his daughter. He is prepared to:

> *"...make a desperate tender of my child's love:"*

His grief for Tybalt's death is not heartfelt. He wishes only to appear grief-stricken and will keep the wedding quiet:

> *"It may be thought we held him carelessly,*
> *Being our kinsman, if we revel much."*

PARIS

Paris wishes to marry Juliet but we have no reason to believe that he loves her. Wooing seems for him a matter of form:

> *"These times of woe afford no times to woo."*

Probably he finds a marriage to Juliet socially desirable.

Scene V

The Same. Juliet's Chamber
Enter Romeo and Juliet

Juliet

Wilt thou be gone? it is not yet near day:
It was the nightingale, and not the lark,
That pierc'd the fearful[1] hollow of thine ear;

[1]frightened

Nightly she sings on yon[2] pomegranate tree:

[2]that

Believe me, love, it was the nightingale.

Romeo

It was the lark, the herald of the morn,
No nightingale: look, love, what envious[3] streaks

[3]malicious

Do lace the severing[4] clouds in yonder east:

[4]parting

Night's candles[5] are burnt out, and jocund day

[5]stars

Stands tiptoe on the misty mountain tops: 10
I must be gone and live, or stay and die.

Juliet

Yon light is not daylight, I know it, I:
It is some meteor that the sun exhales,
To be to thee this night a torch-bearer,
And light thee on thy way to Mantua:
Therefore stay yet; thou need'st not to be gone.

Romeo

Let me be ta'en, let me be put to death;
I am content, so thou wilt have it so.
I'll say yon grey is not the morning's eye,
'Tis but the pale reflex of Cynthia's[6] brow;   20

[6]the moon's reflection

Nor that is not the lark, whose notes do beat
The vaulty heaven so high above our heads:
I have more care[7] to stay than will to go:

[7]I would prefer

Come, death, and welcome! Juliet wills it so.
How is't, my soul? let's talk; it is not day.

Juliet

It is, it is; hie hence, be gone, away!
It is the lark that sings so out of tune,
Straining harsh discords and unpleasing sharps.
Some say the lark makes sweet division;[8]

[8]music

This doth not so, for she divideth us: 30
Some say the lark and loathed toad change eyes;
O! now I would they had chang'd voices too,
Since arm from arm that voice doth us affray,[9]

[9]frighten

[10]hunter's morning song

Hunting thee hence with hunts-up[10] to the day.
O! now be gone; more light and light it grows.

Romeo

More light and light; more dark and dark our woes.

Enter Nurse

Nurse

Madam!

Juliet

Nurse!

Nurse

Your lady mother is coming to your chamber:
The day is broke; be wary, look about.   *[Exit* 40

Juliet

Then, window, let day in, and let life out.

Romeo

Farewell, farewell! one kiss, and I'll descend.

[Descends

Juliet

Art thou gone so? love, lord, ay husband, friend!
I must hear from thee every day in the hour,
For in a minute there are many days:
[11]much older   O! by this count I shall be much in years[11]
Ere I again behold my Romeo.

Romeo

Farewell!
I will omit no opportunity
That may convey my greetings, love, to thee.   50

Juliet

O! think'st thou we shall ever meet again?

Romeo

I doubt it not; and all these woes shall serve
For sweet discourses in our time to come.

Juliet

[12]foreseeing evil   O God! I have an ill-divining[12] soul:
Methinks I see thee, now thou art so low.
As one dead in the bottom of a tomb:
Either my eyesight fails, or thou look'st pale.

Romeo

And trust me, love, in my eye so do you:
Dry sorrow drinks our blood. Adieu! adieu!   *[Exit*

Juliet

O fortune, fortune! all men call thee fickle: *60*
If thou art fickle, what dost thou with him
That is renown'd for faith? Be fickle, fortune;
For then, I hope, thou wilt not keep him long,
But send him back.

Lady Capulet *[Within]*

Ho, daughter! are you up?

Juliet

Who is't that calls? is it my lady mother?
Is she not down so late, or up so early?
What unaccustom'd cause procures[13] her hither?   [13]brings

Enter Lady Capulet

Lady Capulet

Why, how now,[14] Juliet!   [14]how are you?

Juliet

                    Madam, I am not well.

Lady Capulet

Evermore weeping for your cousin's death?   *70*
What! wilt thou wash him from his grave with tears?
And if thou couldst, thou couldst not make him live;
Therefore, have done; some grief shows much of
          love;
But much of grief shows still some want of wit.

Juliet

Yet let me weep for such a feeling loss.

Lady Capulet

So shall you feel the loss, but not the friend
Which you weep for.

Juliet

                    Feeling so the loss,
I cannot choose but ever weep the friend.

Lady Capulet

Well, girl, thou weep'st not so much for his death,
As that the villain lives which slaughter'd him.   *80*

Juliet

What villain, madam?

Lady Capulet

                    That same villain, Romeo.

Juliet *[Aside]*
Villain and he be many miles asunder.
God pardon him! I do, with all my heart;
And yet no man like he doth grieve my heart.

Lady Capulet
That is because the traitor murderer lives.

Juliet
Ay, madam, from the reach of these my hands.
Would none but I might venge my cousin's death!

Lady Capulet
We will have vengeance for it, fear thou not:
Then weep no more. I'll send to one in Mantua,
Where that same banish'd runagate[15] doth live,   *90*
Shall give him such an unaccustom'd dram[16]
That he shall soon keep Tybalt company:
And then, I hope, thou wilt be satisfied.

Juliet
Indeed, I never shall be satisfied
With Romeo, till I behold him — dead —
Is my poor heart so for a kinsman vex'd:
Madam, if you could find out but a man
To bear a poison, I would temper[17] it,
That Romeo should, upon receipt thereof,
Soon sleep in quiet. O! how my heart abhors   *100*
To hear him nam'd, and cannot come to him,
To wreak the love I bore my cousin Tybalt
Upon his body that hath slaughter'd him.

Lady Capulet
Find thou the means, and I'll find such a man.
But now I'll tell thee joyful tidings, girl.

Juliet
And joy comes well in such a needy time:
What are they, I beseech your ladyship?

Lady Capulet
Well, well, thou hast a careful father, child;
One who, to put thee from thy heaviness,
Hath sorted out a sudden day of joy   *110*
That thou expect'st not, nor look'd not for.

Juliet
Madam, in happy time, what day is that?

[15]renegade
[16]poison

[17]mix, weaken

Lady Capulet

Marry, my child, early next Thursday morn
The gallant, young, and noble gentleman,
The County Paris, at Saint Peter's church,
Shall happily make thee there a joyful bride.

Juliet

Now, by Saint Peter's church, and Peter too,
He shall not make me there a joyful bride.
I wonder at this haste; that I must wed
Ere he that should be husband comes to woo.   *120*
I pray you, tell my lord and father, madam,
I will not marry yet; and, when I do, I swear,
It shall be Romeo, whom you know I hate,
Rather than Paris. These are news indeed!

Lady Capulet

Here comes your father; tell him so yourself,
And see how he will take it at your hands.

Enter Capulet and Nurse

Capulet

When the sun sets, the air doth drizzle dew;
But for the sunset of my brother's son
It rains downright.
How now! a conduit,[18] girl? what! still in tears?   *130*   [18]tears (water-pipe)
Evermore showering? In one little body
Thou counterfeit'st a bark,[19] a sea, a wind;   [19]boat
For still thy eyes, which I may call the sea,
Do ebb and flow with tears; the bark thy body is,
Sailing in this salt flood; the winds, thy sighs;
Who, raging with thy tears, and they with them,
Without a sudden calm, will overset[20]   [20]overturn
Thy tempest-tossed body. How now, wife!
Have you deliver'd to her our decree?

Lady Capulet

Ay, sir; but she will none, she gives you thanks.   *140*
I would the fool were married to her grave!

Capulet

Soft! take me with you, take me with you,[21] wife.   [21]help me to understand
How! will she none? doth she not give us thanks?
Is she not proud? doth she not count her bless'd,
Unworthy as she is, that we have wrought[22]   [22]arranged
So worthy a gentleman to be her bridegroom?

Juliet

Not proud, you have; but thankful, that you have:
Proud can I never be of what I hate;
But thankful even for hate, that is meant love.

Capulet

How now! how now! chop-logic!²³ What is this?   *150*
'Proud,' and 'I thank you,' and 'I thank you not;'
And yet 'not proud;' mistress minion,²⁴ you,
Thank me no thankings, nor proud me no prouds,
But fettle²⁵ your fine joints 'gainst Thursday next,
To go with Paris to Saint Peter's church,
Or I will drag thee on a hurdle²⁶ thither.
Out, you green-sickness carrion!²⁷ out! you
        baggage!
You tallow face!²⁸

Lady Capulet

            Fie, fie! what, are you mad?

Juliet

Good father, I beseech you on my knees,
Hear me with patience but to speak a word.   *160*

Capulet

Hang thee, young baggage! disobedient wretch!
I tell thee what, get thee to church o' Thursday,
Or never after look me in the face.
Speak not, reply not, do not answer me;
My fingers itch. — Wife, we scarce thought us
        bless'd
That God had lent us but this only child;
But now I see this one is one too much,
And that we have a curse in having her.
Out on her, hilding!²⁹

Nurse

            God in heaven bless her!
You are to blame, my lord, to rate³⁰ her so.   *170*

Capulet

And why, my lady wisdom? hold your tongue,
Good prudence; smatter³¹ with your gossips, go.

Nurse

I speak no treason.

Capulet

            O! God ye good den.

²³quibbling

²⁴minx

²⁵get ready

²⁶sledge, cart
²⁷pale corpse

²⁸pale face

²⁹worthless girl

³⁰scold

³¹chatter

Nurse
May not one speak?

Capulet

          Peace, you mumbling fool;
Utter your gravity[32] 'er a gossip's bowl;   [32]wisdom
For here we need it not.

Lady Capulet

          You are too hot.

Capulet
God's bread! it makes me mad.
Day, night, hour, tide, time, work, play,
Alone, in company, still my care hath been
To have her match'd; and having now provided   *180*
A gentleman of noble parentage,
Of fair demesnes,[33] youthful, and nobly train'd,   [33]estates
Stuff'd, as they say, wth honourable parts,
Proportion'd as one's thought would wish a man;
And then to have a wretched puling fool,
A whining mammet[34] in her fortune's tender,[35]   [34]puppet
To answer 'I'll not wed,' 'I cannot love,'   [35]offered good fortune
'I am too young,' 'I pray you, pardon me;'
But, an[36] you will not wed, I'll pardon you: [36]if
Graze where you will, you shall not house with me: *190*
Look to 't, think on 't, I do not use to jest.
Thursday is near; lay hand on heart, advise.
An you be mine, I'll give you to my friend;
An you be not, hang, beg, starve, die in the streets,
For, by my soul, I'll ne'er acknowledge thee,
Nor what is mine shall never do thee good.
Trust to't, bethink you; I'll not be forsworn.   *[Exit*

Juliet
Is there no pity sitting in the clouds,
That sees into the bottom of my grief?
O! sweet my mother, cast me not away: *200*
Delay this marriage for a month, a week;
Or, if you do not, make the bridal bed
In that dim monument where Tybalt lies.

Lady Capulet
Talk not to me, for I'll not speak a word.
Do as thou wilt, for I have done with thee.   *[Exit*

Juliet
O God! O nurse! how shall this be prevented?
My husband is on earth, my faith in heaven;

How shall that faith return again to earth,
Unless that husband send it me from heaven
By leaving earth? comfort me, counsel me.   *210*
Alack, alack! that heaven should practise
                    stratagems[37]
Upon so soft[38] a subject as myself!
What sayst thou? hast thou not a word of joy?
Some comfort, nurse?

Nurse

                              Faith, here it is. Romeo
Is banished; and all the world to nothing
That he dares ne'er come back to challenge you;
Or, if he do, it needs must be by stealth.
Then, since the case so stands as now it doth,
I think it best you married with the county.
O! he's a lovely gentleman;   *220*
Romeo's a dishclout[39] to him: an eagle, madam,
Hath not so green, so quick, so fair an eye
As Paris hath. Beshrew[40] my very heart,
I think you are happy in this second match,
For it excels your first: or if it did not,
Your first is dead; or 'twere as good he were,
As living here and you no use of him.

Juliet

Speakest thou from thy heart?

Nurse

                              And from my soul too;
Or else beshrew them both.

Juliet

                    Amen!

Nurse

                    What!

Juliet

Well, thou hast comforted me marvellous much.   *230*
Go in; and tell my lady I am gone,
Having displeas'd my father, to Laurence' cell,
To make confession and to be absolv'd.

Nurse

Marry, I will; and this is wisely done.   [*Exit*

Juliet

Ancient damnation! O most wicked fiend!
Is it more sin to wish me thus forsworn,

[37]cunning schemes

[38]defenceless

[39]dishcloth

[40]curse

Or to dispraise my lord with that same tongue
Which she hath prais'd him with above compare
So many thousand times? Go, counsellor;
Thou and my bosom henceforth shall be twain.[41]   *240*   [41]separated
I'll to the friar, to know his remedy:
If all else fail, myself have power to die.   *[Exit*

Summary – Time: At dawn on Tuesday morning

The Lovers' Farewell

Dawn approaches and the awakening lovers prepare to say farewell for Romeo must flee to Mantua as the Prince decreed. Juliet is unwilling to part from Romeo and he welcomes death if that is Juliet's wish. Juliet realises he must leave her.

The nurse warns that Lady Capulet is coming and Romeo goes down the balcony and the lovers part forever. Romeo tries to be hopeful for the future, but Juliet has premonitions of their deaths. Romeo bravely leaves her for the last time alive.

Juliet is Isolated

Juliet goes to her mother sadly, who advises her not to mourn so much for Tybalt's death. Lady Capulet desires to poison Romeo in vengeance for his murder of Tybalt. Juliet wishes Romeo dead, but so that he may have peace from his sufferings.

Then Lady Capulet tells Juliet that her loving father has arranged a wonderful marriage for her with Paris on the following Thursday, a day of joy. Juliet is shocked and flatly refuses to marry Paris.

Capulet enters and is angry at Juliet's disobedience. His fury increases and shocks both the nurse and Lady Capulet by its violence. Juliet begs him to listen to her, but he retorts that he will disown her if she refuses to marry as he wishes. He storms out of the room feeling betrayed by the daughter he tried to please.

Juliet turns to her mother for sympathy, but her mother dismisses her coldly. In desperation, Juliet turns to the nurse who advises that one man is as good as another and she should marry Paris. Juliet is disgusted with the nurse.

Juliet is now on her own and decides to seek Friar Laurence's help and, if that fails, she intends to die.

Scene Analysis

A Farewell to Love

This scene is the last time we see the lovers alive together. They have spent a blissful night together and are unwilling to end it. For a brief moment, their happiness knows no bounds:

> *"I have more care to stay than will to go:"*   *(Romeo)*

> *"Therefore stay yet; thou need'st not to be gone."*   *(Juliet)*

Art thou gone so? love, lord, ay husband, friend!   *(Juliet, Act 3 Scene V)*

This contrasts sharply with the rest of the scene, which is full of violence, misunderstandings and anger.

Despite their bliss, the lovers realise that their happiness will be short-lived in the harsh circumstances that return with the dawn light. Romeo is afraid for his safety:

> *"I must be gone and live, or stay and die."*

Juliet foresees Romeo's death:

> *"Methinks I see thee, now thou art so low.*
> *As one dead in the bottom of a tomb:"*

Romeo tries to be optimistic:

> *"...all these woes shall serve*
> *For sweet discourses in our time to come."*

But we are left in no doubt that tragedy is approaching swiftly due to fateful circumstances outside the lovers' control:

> *"Alack, alack! that heaven should practise stratagems*
> *Upon so soft a subject as myself!"*

The Violent World Closes In

Lady Capulet wishes Romeo dead and informs Juliet of her coming marriage to Paris. She becomes the instrument of hate and social pressure, which tries to manipulate Juliet's future. Juliet is caught between fidelity to her marriage of love to Romeo and loyalty and obedience to her family. There seems no way out but death. Ironically, Juliet says:

> *"Indeed, I never shall be satisfied*
> *With Romeo, till I behold him — dead. —"*

Juliet's father believes that marriage to Paris is best for Juliet's future security. He does not realise that Juliet has already married for love. In a violent quarrel, Capulet, disappointed at his daughter's disloyalty to him and her family, disowns her:

> *"An you be mine, I'll give you to my friend;*
> *An you be not, hang, beg, starve, die in the streets,*
> *For, by my soul, I'll ne'er acknowledge thee,"*

I tell thee what, get thee to church o' Thursday,
or never after look me in the face.   (Capulet, Act 3, Scene V)

All hope of her father's understanding has gone.

Juliet's mother is unsympathetic:

> *"Do as thou wilt, for I have done with thee."*

Even her confidante, the nurse, fails to understand Juliet's predicament.

> *"I think it best you married with the county.*
> *O! he's a lovely gentleman;*
> *Romeo's a dishclout to him:"*

Juliet is disgusted at the nurse's immoral suggestions. Isolated from family and friend, Juliet sees no way out of her dilemma except death:

> *"If all else fail, myself have power to die."*

Characters

JULIET

Juliet displays heroic qualities in her confrontation with her parents. She has attained a new maturity of character through her love for Romeo. Under extreme pressure, she courageously defies her parents' wishes:

> *'Now, by Saint Peter's church, and Peter too,*
> *He shall not make me there a joyful bride."*

She is calm and determined with her furious father:

> *"Good father, I beseech you on my knees,*
> *Hear me with patience but to speak a word."*

When the nurse betrays her, she does not take the easy way out but will die if all else fails:

> *"If all else fail, myself have power to die."*

On her own she will confront her destiny.

Juliet is as tender and loving as she is heroic and determined. She loves Romeo with all her soul:

> *"God pardon him! I do, with all my heart;*
> *And yet no man like he doth grieve my heart."*

CAPULET

In normal circumstances, Capulet is a kindly, affectionate father:

> *"How now! a conduit, girl? what! still in tears?"*

He has tried to do his best to secure Juliet's happiness and cannot understand why she rejects his efforts:

> *"Is she not proud? doth she not count her bless'd,*
> *Unworthy as she is, that we have wrought*
> *So worthy a gentleman to be her bridegroom?"*

Capulet, however well intentioned, becomes a heavy-handed tyrant when confronted with his defiant daughter. He threatens and insults her and is ready to strike her for her disobedience. However, his only real fault is his failure to listen to the explanation of his kneeling daughter:

> *"Hang thee, young baggage! disobedient wretch!"*

Overall his conduct is no worse than was to be expected in Shakespeare's time, when fathers were absolute masters in their own households.

LADY CAPULET

As in the crisis scene, Lady Capulet is eager for vengeance, blood for blood:

> *"We will have vengeance for it, fear thou not:"*

She, more than anyone else, keeps the feud going.

Lady Capulet is a status-seeker who has little real affection for her daughter. When Juliet refuses to fall in with her plans to increase their social standing, she coldly deserts Juliet in her hour of need:

> *"Talk not to me, for I'll not speak a word.*
> *Do as thou wilt, for I have done with thee."*

THE NURSE

The nurse really cares for Juliet. She risks her own position to defend Juliet against her father:

> *"God in heaven bless her!*
> *"You are to blame, my lord, to rate her so."*

The nurse misunderstands Juliet's real love for Romeo. She advises Juliet to enter into an immoral and illegal marriage with Paris. Juliet is disgusted:

> *"Ancient damnation! O most wicked fiend!*
> *"It is more sin to wish me thus forsworn,"*

Act 4
Scene I

Verona. Friar Laurence's Cell
Enter Friar Laurence and Paris

Friar Laurence
On Thursday, sir? the time is very short.

Paris
My father Capulet will have it so;
And I am nothing slow to slack[1] his haste.

Friar Laurence
You say you do not know the lady's mind:
Uneven[2] is the course, I like it not.

Paris
Immoderately she weeps for Tybalt's death,
And therefore have I little talk of love;
For Venus smiles not in a house of tears.
Now, sir, her father counts it dangerous
That she doth give her sorrow so much sway,[3]   *10*
And in his wisdom hastes our marriage
To stop the inundation of her tears;
Which, too much minded[4] by herself alone,
May be put from her by society.
Now do you know the reason of this haste.

Friar Laurence *[Aside]*
I would I knew not why it should be slow'd.
Look, sir, here comes the lady towards my cell.

Enter Juliet

Paris
Happily met, my lady and my wife!

Juliet
That may be, sir, when I may be a wife.

Paris
That may be must be, love, on Thursday next.   *20*

Juliet
What must be shall be.

Friar Laurence
                              That's a certain text.

Paris
Come you to make confession to this father?

---

[1]check, delay

[2]strange

[3]influence

[4]thought of

Juliet
To answer that, I should confess to you.

Paris
Do not deny to him that you love me.

Juliet
I will confess to you that I love him.

Paris
So will ye, I am sure, that you love me.

Juliet
If I do so, it will be of more price,
Being spoke behind your back, than to your face.

Paris
Poor soul, thy face is much abus'd with tears.

Juliet
The tears have got small victory by that;   30
For it was bad enough before their spite.

Paris
Thou wrong'st it, more than tears, with that report.[5]   [5]criticism

Juliet
That is no slander, sir, which is a truth;
And what I spake, I spake it to my face.

Paris
Thy face is mine, and thou hast slander'd it.

Juliet
It may be so, for it is not mine own.
Are you at leisure, holy father, now;
Or shall I come to you at evening mass?

Friar Laurence
My leisure serves me, pensive daughter, now:
My lord, we must entreat[6] the time alone.   40   [6]ask for

Paris
God shield,[7] I should disturb devotion!   [7]God forbid
Juliet, on Thursday early will I rouse ye:
Till then, adieu; and keep this holy kiss.   [Exit

Juliet
O! shut the door! and when thou hast done so,
Come weep with me; past hope, past care, past
        help!

Friar Laurence
O! Juliet, I already know thy grief;
It strains me past the compass[8] of my wits: [8]limit
I hear thou must, and nothing may prorogue[9] it,   [9]delay
On Thursday next be married to this county.

Juliet
Tell me not, friar, that thou hear'st of this,   *50*
Unless thou tell me how I may prevent it:
If, in thy wisdom, thou canst give no help,
Do thou but call my resolution wise,
And with this knife I'll help it presently.
God join'd my heart and Romeo's, thou our hands;
And ere this hand, by thee to Romeo seal'd,
Shalf be the label[10] to another deed,
Or my true heart with treacherous revolt
Turn to another, this shall slay them both.
Therefore, out of thy long-experienc'd time,   *60*
Give me some present counsel; or behold,
'Twixt my extremes and me this bloody knife
Shall play the umpire, arbitrating that
Which the commission[11] of thy years and art
Could to no issue of true honour bring.
Be not so long to speak; I long to die,
If what thou speak'st speak not of remedy.

Friar Laurence
Hold, daughter; I do spy a kind of hope,
Which craves as desperate an execution
As that is desperate which we would prevent.   *70*
If, rather than to marry County Paris,
Thou hast the strength of will to slay thyself,
Then is it likely thou wilt undertake
A thing like death to chide away this shame,
That cop'st with death himself to 'scape from it;
And, if thou dar'st, I'll give thee remedy.

Juliet
O! bid me leap, rather than marry Paris,
From off the battlements of any tower;
Or walk in thievish ways; or bid me lurk
Where serpents are; chain me with roaring bears;   *80*
Or hide me nightly in a charnel-house,
O'er cover'd quite with dead men's rattling bones,
With reeky[12] shanks, and yellow chapless[13] skulls;
Or bid me go into a new-made grave
And hide me with a dead man in his shroud;
Things that, to hear them told, have made me
         tremble;
And I will do it without fear or doubt,
To live an unstain'd wife to my sweet love.

[10]seal

[11]authority

[12]damp
[13]jawless

This foreshadows what's to come

Friar Laurence

Hold, then; go home, be merry, give consent
To marry Paris: Wednesday is to-morrow: 90
To-morrow night look that thou lie alone,
Let not thy nurse lie with thee in thy chamber:
Take thou this vial, being then in bed,
And this distilled liquor drink thou off;
When presently through all thy veins shall run
A cold and drowsy humour,[14] for no pulse   [14] fluid
Shall keep his native progress,[15] but surcease;[16]   [15] natural movement
No warmth, no breath, shall testify thou liv'st;   [16] stop
The roses in thy lips and cheeks shall fade
To paly ashes; thy eyes' windows fall,   100
Like death, when he shuts up the day of life;
Each part, depriv'd of supple government,[17]   [17] ability to move
Shall, stiff and stark and cold, appear like death;
And in this borrow'd likeness of shrunk death
Thou shalt continue two-and-forty hours,
And then awake as from a pleasant sleep.
Now, when the bridegroom in the morning comes
To rouse thee from thy bed, there art thou dead:
Then — as the manner of our country is —
In thy best robes uncover'd on the bier,   110
Thou shalt be borne to that same ancient vault
Where all the kindred of the Capulets lie.
In the mean time, against[18] thou shalt awake   [18] in preparation for
Shall Romeo by my letters know our drift,[19]   [19] plan
And hither shall he come; and he and I
Will watch thy waking, and that very night
Shall Romeo bear thee hence to Mantua.
And this shall free thee from this present shame;
If no unconstant toy, nor womanish fear,
Abate[20] thy valour in the acting it.   120   [20] lessen

Juliet

Give me, give me! O! tell me not of fear!

Friar Laurence

Hold; get you gone, be strong and prosperous[21]   [21] successful
In this resolve. I'll send a friar with speed
To Mantua, with my letters to thy lord.

Juliet

Love, give me strength! and strength shall help
        afford.
Farewell, dear father!   [*Exeunt*

Summary – Time: Tuesday morning

A Desperate Remedy

In Friar Laurence's cell, Paris is arranging for his marriage on the following Thursday. The friar is shocked at the haste and Paris explains that Capulet wishes an early marriage to put an end to Juliet's sadness at Tybalt's death.

Juliet arrives and in her conversation with Paris avoids betraying Romeo or rejecting Paris. Paris leaves, thinking Juliet has come to give her confession to the friar.

Alone with the friar, Juliet confesses her desperation and the friar brings no solution to her problem. Juliet is determined to kill herself if she cannot avoid the marriage to Paris.

Seeing her hopelessness, the friar invents a plan. The night before the wedding, Juliet must take a drug which the friar gives her. This drug will make her sleep for forty-two hours, after which she will awaken unharmed. Her family will then lay her in the Capulet tomb and the friar will call Romeo from Mantua to take Juliet away with him.

Juliet gladly agrees to this plan and the friar promises to send a message to Romeo straight away.

Scene Analysis

The Friar's Tragic Plan

Juliet is desperate. She sees no means of avoiding the marriage to Paris except suicide. She is *"past hope, past cure, past help!"* As a last resort she has come to the friar for help. If he cannot help she intends to kill herself for love:

> *"Do thou but call my resolution wise,*
> *And with this knife I'll help it presently."*

All seems hopeless for Juliet.

The well-meaning friar hastily invents a plan to prevent Juliet's suicide. If it works the lovers will be together again; if it fails tragedy will result. Juliet, in a courageous act of love, grasps at this last chance of happiness, whatever the risks:

> *"Love, give me strength! and strength shall help afford."*

Juliet gives all for love and we hope against hope she will win through.

This scene presents us with an emergency situation, calling for desperate remedies. Minute by minute the situation is worsening. Romeo is banished on pain of death and Juliet confronts an immoral marriage just days away. She has no one to help her except the kindly friar. Father, mother, nurse – all have deserted her. Time is running out. The demands of society and Fate have isolated her from the love she lives for and will die for. The play hastens towards a tragic end.

I'll send a friar with speed
To Mantua, with letters to thy lord.

(Friar Laurence, Act 4, Scene I)

Characters

JULIET

Juliet shows heroic strength in her determination *"to live an unstain'd wife to my sweet love"*. Her loyalty to her husband lends her new courage. She will give all for her fidelity:

> *"O! bid me leap, rather than marry Paris,*
> *From off the battlements of any tower."*

Juliet sees herself as *"past hope, past cure, past help!"*, but she never loses control of herself. She can still retain a sense of humour as she speaks to Paris.

> *"The tears have got small victory by that;*
> *For it was bad enough before their spite."*

THE FRIAR

As before, the friar is sympathetic and well-meaning. He uses his knowledge of drugs to help Juliet in distress, even though he knows the risks involved are great. Seeing Juliet's despondency, he reaches out to her:

> *"Hold daughter; I do spy a kind of hope,*
> *Which craves as desperate an execution*
> *As that is desperate which we would prevent."*

He never stops to think of the direct approach of telling the truth to the families and trying to reconcile them.

PARIS

As before, Paris is a conventional, gentlemanly suitor who is conscious of his social position and desires a marriage worthy of his standing. He has little real affection for Juliet:

> *"And therefore have I little talk of love;*
> *For Venus smiles not in a house of tears."*

Juliet is glad when he leaves:

> *"O! shut the door!..."*

Scene II

The Same. Hall in Capulet's House
Enter Capulet, Lady Capulet Nurse, and Servingmen

Capulet
So many guests invite as here are writ.

[*Exit Servant*

Sirrah, go hire me twenty cunning[1] cooks.   [1]skilful

Second Servingman
You shall have none ill,[2] sir; for I'll try if they can lick   [2]bad
their fingers.

Capulet
How canst thou try them so?

Second Servingman
Marry, sir, 'tis an ill cook that cannot lick his own
fingers: therefore he that cannot lick his fingers
goes not with me.

Capulet
Go, be gone.   [*Exit Second Servant*
We shall be much unfurnish'd[3] for this time.   10   [3]unprepared
What! is my daughter gone to Friar Laurence?

Nurse
Ay, forsooth.

Capulet
Well, he may chance to do some good on her:
A peevish self-will'd harlotry it is.

Nurse
See where she comes from shrift with merry look.

Enter Juliet

Capulet
How now, my headstrong! where have you been
    gadding?[4]   [4]wandering

Juliet
Where I have learn'd me to repent the sin
Of disobedient opposition
To you and your behests;[5] and am enjoin'd[6]   [5]orders
By holy Laurence to fall prostrate here,   20   [6]compelled
And beg your pardon. Pardon, I beseech you!
Henceforward I am ever rul'd by you.

Capulet

Send for the county; go tell him of this:

I'll have this knot knit up to-morrow morning.

Juliet

I met the youthful lord at Laurence' cell;

And gave him what becomed[7] love I might,

Not stepping o'er the bounds of modesty.

Capulet

Why, I'm glad on 't, this is well: stand up:

This is as 't should be. Let me see the county;

Ay, marry, go, I say, and fetch him hither.   30

Now, afore God! this reverend holy friar,

All our whole city is much bound to him.

Juliet

Nurse, will you go with me into my closet.[8]

To help me sort such needful ornaments

As you think fit to furnish me to-morrow?

Lady Capulet

No, not till Thursday; there is time enough.

Capulet

Go, nurse, go with her. We'll to church to-morrow.

> [Exeunt Juliet and Nurse

Lady Capulet

We shall be short in our provision:

'Tis now near night.

Capulet

                        Tush! I will stir about,[9]

And all things shall be well, I warrant thee, wife: 40

Go thou to Juliet, help to deck up her;

I'll not to bed to-night; let me alone;

I'll play the housewife for this once. What, ho!

They are all forth: well, I will walk myself

To County Paris, to prepare up him

Against[10] to-morrow. My heart is wondrous light,

Since this same wayward girl is so reclaim'd.

> [Exeunt

[Handwritten note: we the audience are surprised and concerned at the sudden change of events and we wonder what implications this will have Juliet and romeo's fate]

7 proper

8 room

9 I will get busy

10 for

Summary – Time: Nightfall on Tuesday

An Early Wedding

At Capulet's house, Capulet is making preparations for the wedding. He is happy and hopes the friar has changed Juliet's attitude.

Juliet enters and asks her father's forgiveness for disobeying his wishes. Capulet is so happy that he advances the wedding to Wednesday, despite his wife's opposition. He decides to go and tell Paris the good news, not realising that Juliet has different intentions.

Scene Analysis

Another Step Towards Tragedy

Juliet carries out the friar's plan exactly in this scene. So successfully does she feign her apology to her father that the wedding is brought forward by a day. It is ironic and tragic that Juliet herself, by her single-mindedness in carrying out the plan, makes the problems even greater. There is now less time to inform Romeo of the plan and the chances of success are lessened.

This short scene emphasises the complete isolation of Juliet from her parents and former confidante, the nurse. Nobody knows of her deception except the friar. She is alone against the world with only her love to guide her.

Characters

JULIET

The absolute proof of Juliet's fidelity to her love is seen in her unflinching and single-minded deception of her family and the nurse. Not a hint does she give of her real intentions, nor does she react to the changing of the day of the wedding:

> *"Henceforward I am ever rul'd by you."*

Her self-control is admirable.

CAPULET

Capulet shows his true character in this scene. He dominates his family and is happy only when he gets his own way. He changes his mind as the whim suits him. He intends an extravagant wedding despite Tybalt's death and changes the day of the wedding on impulse:

> *'This is as 't should be,"*

he says when Juliet apologises for being *"headstrong"*.

Scene III

The Same. Juliet's Chamber
Enter Juliet and Nurse

Juliet

Ay, those attires are best; but gentle nurse,
I pray thee, leave me to myself to-night;
For I have need of many orisons[1]
To move the heavens to smile upon my state,
Which, well thou know'st, is cross[2] and full of sin.

Enter Lady Capulet

Lady Capulet

What! are you busy, ho? need you my help?

Juliet

No, madam; we have cull'd[3] such necessaries
As are behoveful[4] for our state[5] to-morrow:
So please you, let me now be left alone,
And let the nurse this night sit up with you;   10
For, I am sure, you have your hands full all
In this so sudden business.

Lady Capulet

          Good-night:
Get thee to bed, and rest; for thou hast need.

        [Exeunt Lady Capulet and Nurse

Juliet

Farewell! God knows when we shall meet again.
I have a faint cold fear thrills through my veins,
That almost freezes up the heat of life:
I'll call them back again to comfort me:
Nurse! What should she do here?
My dismal scene I needs must act alone.
Come, vial.   20
What if this mixture do not work at all?
Shall I be married then to-morrow morning?
No, no; this shall forbid it: lie thou there.

        [Laying down a dagger

What if it be a poison, which the friar
Subtly hath minister'd to have me dead,
Lest in this marriage he should be dishonour'd
Because he married me before to Romeo?
I fear it is: and yet, methinks, it should not,

[1] prayers

[2] perverse

[3] chosen
[4] needed
[5] pomp and ceremony

Dagger is placed beside her to react

2

For he hath still[6] been tried[7] a holy man.

I will not entertain so bad a thought.   *30*

How if, when I am laid into the tomb,

I wake before the time that Romeo

Come to redeem me? there's a fearful point!

Shall I not then be stifled in the vault?

To whose foul mouth no health some air breathes
        in,

And there die strangled ere my Romeo comes?

Or, if I live, is it not very like,

The horrible conceit[8] of death and night,

Together with the terror of the place,

As in a vault, an ancient receptacle,[9]   *40*

Where, for these many hundred years, the bones

Of all my buried ancestors are pack'd;

Where bloody Tybalt, yet but green in earth,

Lies festering in his shroud; where, as they say,

At some hours in the night spirits resort:[10]

Alack, alack! is it not like that I,

So early waking, what with loathsome smells,

And shrieks like mandrakes'[11] torn out of the earth;

That living mortals, hearing them, run mad:

O! if I wake, shall I not be distraught,[12]   *50*

Environed[13] with all these hideous fears,

And madly play with my forefathers' joints,

And pluck the mangled Tybalt from his shroud?

And, in this rage, with some great kinsman's bone,

As with a club, dash out of my desperate brains?

O look! methinks I see my cousin's ghost

Seeking out Romeo, that did spit[14] his body

Upon a rapier's point. Stay, Tybalt, stay!

Romeo, I come! this do I drink to thee.

[She falls upon her bed within the curtains

[6]always
[7]proven
[8]thought
[9]burial place
[10]rest
[11]shrieking plant
[12]driven mad
[13]surrounded
[14]pierce

Summary – Time: Tuesday night

Juliet's Sacrifice

In her room, Juliet arranges her clothes and sends away the nurse. Lady Capulet is also dismissed so that Juliet can take the friar's sleep-inducing drug a day earlier than planned.

As Juliet holds the drug, one fear after another flashes through her mind. Will the drug work at all? Perhaps it is a poison given by the friar to save him from disgrace? She imagines the horrors of waking up too soon in the stifling vault among the ghosts of her ancestors.

Finally she swallows the drug for Romeo's sake and falls asleep on her bed.

Scene Analysis

A Love Stronger than Death Itself

Juliet trusts absolutely to the power of her love in this scene. She is determined to die for love and has her dagger at hand in case the drug fails. She is not sure that the friar did not give her poison to save his reputation. She imagines the terror of awaking too soon in the vault only to be stifled for lack of air. Worst of all she imagines the horror of lying among rotting bodies and unearthly spirits.

Yet Juliet takes the drug despite all these terrors. She sacrifices herself to the one ideal that matters, her love. In a sense, Juliet's love overcomes death and transcends it in this scene. Shakespeare asserts the absolute value of love through Juliet's sacrifice.

"Romeo, I come! this do I drink to thee."

How if, when I am laid into the tomb,
I wake before the time that Romeo
Come to redeem me? There's a fearful point!   *(Juliet, Act 4, Scene III)*

Characters

JULIET

Juliet attains the status of a tragic heroine in this scene. She confronts forces greater than herself in this scene, trusting to the power of her love to save her:

> *"Romeo, I come! this do I drink to thee."*

She defies the hatred and misfortune of the world and takes on death. Her love for Romeo is greater than her horror of death.

> *"Shall I not then be stifled in the vault?"*

She is determined to die rather than betray her love if the plan fails:

"No, no; this shall forbid it: lie thou there" she says as she lays aside the dagger. We not only sympathise but admire Juliet's heroic traits of character.

Scene IV

The Same. Hall in Capulet's House
Enter Lady Capulet and Nurse

Lady Capulet
Hold, take these keys, and fetch more spices,
    nurse.

Nurse
They call for dates and quinces in the pastry.[1]

                Enter Capulet

Capulet
Come, stir, stir, stir! the second cock hath crow'd,
The curfew bell hath rung, 'tis three o'clock:
Look to the bak'd meats, good Angelica:
Spare not for cost.

Nurse
           Go, go, you cot-quean,[2] go;
Get you to bed; faith, you'll be sick to-morrow
For this night's watching.

Capulet
No, not a whit; what! I have watch'd ere now
All night for lesser cause, and ne'er been sick.   *10*

[1] part of a kitchen

[2] man who does woman's work

³chasing women

Lady Capulet
Ay, you have been a mouse-hunt³ in your time;
But I will watch you from such watching now.
                              [*Exeunt Lady Capulet and Nurse*

Capulet
⁴person
A jealous-hood, a jealous-hood!⁴
      Enter three or four Servingmen, with spits, logs and baskets
                                    Now, fellow,
What's there?

First Servingman
Things for the cook, sir; but I know not what.

Capulet
Make haste, make haste.   [*Exit first Servingman*
Sirrah, fetch drier logs:
Call Peter, he will show thee where they are.

Second Servingman
I have a head, sir, that will find out logs,
And never trouble Peter for the matter.   *20* [*Exit*

Capulet
⁵By the Mass
⁶idiot
Mass,⁵ and well said; a merry whoreson, ha!
Thou shalt be logger-head.⁶ Good faith! 'tis day:
The county will be here with music straight,
For so he said he would. *[Music within]* I hear him
          near.
Nurse! Wife! what, ho! What, nurse, I say!

                    Re-enter Nurse

⁷dress
Go waken Juliet, go and trim⁷ her up;
I'll go and chat with Paris. Hie, make haste,
Make haste; the bridegroom he is come already:
Make haste, I say.

                                        [*Exeunt*

Summary – Time: The early hours of Wednesday morning

Preparations for the Feast

The members of Capulet household, in gay and festive mood, prepare busily for the forthcoming celebrations, unaware, as yet, that their joy will be short-lived. It is to be a feast to remember. Capulet hurries up the preparations, enjoying his late-night adventure. Suddenly the bridegroom arrives and the nurse is sent to awaken Juliet.

Scene Analysis

A Moment of Relief

This light-hearted scene provides temporary relief from the terror of the previous scene and contrasts sharply with the outbursts of grief in the following scene. The comedy of the bustling Capulet household relieves the tension and prepares us for the tragic events to follow.

A Moment of Suspense

Juliet has taken the friar's mixture and we have yet to discover whether she is dead or just asleep. The delay intensifies our suspense since we know that something tragic is about to happen and we wish to discover the details. This suspense is further heightened by the irony of the scene itself. The Capulet household's elaborate plans will come to nothing and they are as yet unaware of this. Such an ironic mood intensifies the tragic events to follow.

Characters

CAPULET

Capulet is enjoying his youthful night-time adventure in an extravagant manner. Everything is as his whims dictate and so he is happy. He will receive a rude awakening from his blindness.

Scene V

The Same. Juliet's Chamber
Enter Nurse

Nurse
Mistress! what, mistress! Juliet! fast,[1] I warrant her,
    she:
Why, lamb! why, lady! fie, you slug-a-bed!
Why, love, I say! madam! sweet-heart! why, bride!
What! not a word? you take your pennyworths
    now:
Sleep for a week; for the next night, I warrant,
The County Paris hath set up his rest
That you shall rest but little. God forgive me,
Marry, and amen, how sound is she asleep!
I needs must wake her. Madam, madam, madam!
Ay, let the county take you in your bed;   *10*
He'll fright you up, i' faith. Will it not be?
What, dress'd! and in your clothes! and down
    again!

[1] asleep

I must needs wake you. Lady! lady! lady!
Alas! alas! Help! help! my lady's dead!
O! well-a-day, that ever I was born.
Some *aqua-vitae*, ho! My lord! my lady!

Enter Lady Capulet

Lady Capulet
What noise is here?

Nurse
                    O lamentable day!

Lady Capulet
What is the matter?

Nurse
                    Look, look! O heavy day!

Lady Capulet
O me, O me! my child, my only life,
Revive, look up, or I will die with thee!   *20*
Help, help! Call help.

Enter Capulet

Capulet
For shame! bring Juliet forth; her lord is come.

Nurse
She's dead, deceas'd, she's dead; alack the day!

Lady Capulet
Alack the day! she's dead, she's dead! she's dead!

Capulet
Ha! let me see her. Out, alas! she's cold;
Her blood is settled, and her joints are stiff;
Life and these lips have long been separated:
Death lies on her like an untimely frost
Upon the sweetest flower of all the field.

Nurse
O lamentable day!

Lady Capulet
                    O woeful time!   *30*

Capulet
Death, that hath ta'en her hence to make me wail,
Ties up my tongue, and will not let me speak.

Enter Friar Laurence, and Paris, with Musicians

Friar Laurence
Come, is the bride ready to go to church?

Capulet
Ready to go, but never to return.
O son! the night before thy wedding-day
Hath Death lain with thy wife. There she lies,
Flower as she was, deflowered by him.
Death is my son-in-law, Death is my heir;
My daughter he hath wedded: I will die,
And leave him all; life, living, all is Death's!   40

Paris
Have I thought long to see this morning's face,
And doth it give me such a sight as this?

Lady Capulet
Accurs'd, unhappy, wretched, hateful day!
Most miserable hour, that e'er time saw
In lasting labour² of his pilgrimage!   ²continual labour
But one, poor one, one poor and loving child,
But one thing to rejoice and solace³ in,   ³comfort
And cruel death hath catch'd⁴ it from my sight!   ⁴snatched

Nurse
O woe! O woeful, woeful, woeful day!
Most lamentable day, most woeful day,   50
That ever, ever, I did yet behold!
O day! O day! O day! O hateful day!
Never was seen so black a day as this:
O woeful day, O woeful day!

Paris
Beguil'd,⁵ divorced, wronged, spited, slain!   ⁵deceived
Most detestable death, by thee beguil'd,
By cruel cruel thee quite overthrown!
O love! O life! not life, but love in death!

Capulet
Despis'd, distressed, hated, martyr'd, kill'd!
Uncomfortable time, why cam'st thou now   60
To murder, murder our solemnity?⁶   ⁶ceremony
O child! O child! my soul, and not my child!
Dead art thou! dead! alack, my child is dead;
And with my child my joys are buried!

Friar Laurence
Peace, ho! for shame! confusion's⁷ cure lives not   ⁷disaster
In these confusions.⁸ Heaven and yourself   ⁸disorder
Had part in this fair maid; now heaven hath all,

And all the better is it for the maid:
Your part[9] in her you could not keep from death,
But heaven keeps his part[10] in eternal life.   70
The most you sought was her promotion,
For 'twas your heaven she should be advanc'd;
And weep ye now, seeing she is advanc'd
Above the clouds, as high as heaven itself?
O! in this love, you love your child so ill,
That you run mad, seeing that she is well:
She's not well married that lives married long;
But she's best married that dies married young.
Dry up your tears, and stick your rosemary[11]
On this fair corse; and, as the custom is,   80
In all her best array bear her to church;
For though fond nature bids us all lament,
Yet nature's tears are reason's merriment.[12]

Capulet

All things that we ordained festival,
Turn from their office to black funeral;
Our instruments to melancholy bells,
Our wedding cheer to a sad burial feast,
Our solemn hymns to sullen dirges change,
Our bridal flowers serve for a buried corse,
And all things change them to the contrary.   90

Friar Laurence

Sir, go you in; and, madam, go with him;
And go, Sir Paris; everyone prepare
To follow this fair corse unto her grave.
The heavens do lower[13] upon you for some ill;
Move them no more by crossing their high will.

        [Exeunt Capulet, Lady Capulet, Paris and Friar

First Musician

Faith, we may put up our pipes, and be gone.

Nurse

Honest good fellows, ah! put up, put up, for, well
you know, this is a pitiful case.   *[Exit*

First Musician

Ay, by my troth, the case may be amended.

        Enter Peter

[9] her body
[10] her soul
[11] a herb of remembrance
[12] a matter of joy for reason
[13] frown

144

Peter

Musicians! O! musicians, 'Heart's ease,   *100*
Heart's ease:' O! an ye will have me live, play
'Heart's ease.'

First Musician

Why 'Heart's ease?'

Peter

O! musicians, because my heart itself plays 'My
heart is full of woe;' O! play me some merry dump,
to comfort me.

Second Musician

Not a dump we; 'tis no time to play now.

Peter

You will not then?

Musicians

No.

Peter

I will then give it you soundly.   *110*

First Musician

What will you give us?

Peter

No money, on my faith! but the gleek;[14] I will give   [14]gibe
you the minstrel.

First Musician

Then will I give you the serving-creature.

Peter

Then will I lay the serving-creature's dagger on   [15]head
your pate,[15] I will carry no crotchets:[16] I'll *re* you,   [16]whims, notes
I'll *fa* you, Do you note me?

First Musician

An you *re* us, and *fa* us, you note us.

Second Musician

Pray you, put up your dagger, and put out your wit.

Peter

Then have at you with my wit! I will dry-beat you   *120*
with an iron wit, and put up my iron dagger. Answer
me like men:

> *When griping grief the heart doth wound,*
> *And doleful dumps the mind oppress,*
> *Then music with her silver sound —*

145

[17]cat-gut (used as a name
   for a musician)

Why 'silver sound?' why 'music with her silver
sound?' What say you, Simon Catling?[17]

First Musician

Marry, sir, because silver hath a sweet sound.

Peter

[18]fiddle

Pretty! What say you, Hugh Rebeck?[18]

Second Musician

I say 'silver sound,' because musicians sound   130
for silver.

Peter

Pretty too! What say you, James Soundpost?

Third Musician

Faith, I know not what to say.

Peter

[19]beg your pardon

O! I cry you mercy;[19] you are the singer; I will say
for you. It is, 'music with her silver sound,' because
musicians have no gold for sounding:
> Then music with her silver sound
> With speedy help doth lend redress.   [Exit

First Musician

What a pestilent knave is this same!

Second Musician

Hang him, Jack! Come, we'll in here; tarry   140
for the mourners, and stay dinner.   [Exeunt

Summary – Time: Tuesday morning directly after Act 4, Scene IV

Juliet is Found Dead

The nurse goes, as instructed, to wake Juliet and calls her affectionate names. The nurse is shocked to find Juliet apparently dead and dressed in her wedding clothes.

The nurse's cries bring the Capulets hurrying to Juliet's bedside and they lament their daughter's untimely death in extravagant exclamations of grief.

Friar Laurence and Paris enter with the musicians for the wedding. Amidst the lamentations of all, the friar pretends to be calm, moralising that Juliet has found advancement to heaven. They should not grieve but must bring her quickly to the church and her tomb. He thus ensures that all happens as he planned.

The scene closes with Peter dismissing the musicians and their comedy reminds us that Juliet's "death" is part of the friar's plan.

Scene Analysis

A Scene of Grief and Relief

This scene dramatically brings to an end the excitement and anticipation of the wedding preparations in the previous scene. Suddenly the discovery of Juliet *"dead"* unleashes a flood of extravagant lamentation from all. We realise that their grief is more conventional than sincere and this emphasises to the audience that the real tragedy has yet to unfold. Friar Laurence makes clear to us that events are happening according to his plan and we have no cause yet for grief:

> "Heaven and yourself
> Had part in this fair maid; now heaven hath all,
> And all the better is it for the maid:"

We hope against hope that the plan will succeed for the lovers' sakes.

Death, that hath ta'en her hence to make me wail,
Ties up my tongue, and will not let me speak.   (Capulet, Act 4, Scene V)

Characters

THE NURSE

The nurse's grief at Juliet's death seems more heartfelt than that of anyone else. She resorts to repetition to overcome her grief at her loss:

> "O woe! O woeful, woeful, woeful day!
> Most lamentable day, most woeful day,
> That ever, ever, I did yet behold!"

PARIS

Paris is concerned with his own loss, showing little pity for Juliet: He is:

> "Beguil'd, divorced, wronged, spited, slain!"

by Juliet's death. He is self-centred.

THE CAPULETS

The Capulets' sorrow for Juliet's death is conventional and insincere. Lady Capulet sees Juliet's death as a loss to her social life:

> "Revive, look up, or I will die with thee!"

Capulet is speechless and feels grief more sincerely than his wife:

> "Death, that hath ta'en her hence to make me wail,
> Ties up my tongue, and will not let me speak."

FRIAR LAURENCE

Friar Laurence is true to his word to Juliet. He carries out his part of the plan forthrightly, giving no hint that Juliet is not dead:

> "Come, is the bride ready to go to church?"

Friar Laurence is critical of the Capulets' attitude to grief and social standing:

> "The most you sought was her promotion,
> For 'twas your heaven she should be advanc'd;
> And weep ye now, seeing she is advanc'd
> Above the clouds, as high as heaven itself?"

Act 5
Scene I

Mantua. A Street. Enter Romeo

Romeo

If I may trust the flattering truth of sleep,[1]
My dreams presage[2] some joyful news at hand:
My bosom's lord[3] sits lightly in his throne;
And all this day an unaccustom'd spirit
Lifts me above the ground with cheerful thoughts.
I dreamt my lady came and found me dead; —
Strange dream, that gives a dead man leave to
        think, —
And breath'd such life with kisses in my lips,
That I reviv'd and was an emperor.
Ah me! how sweet is love itself possess'd,   10
When but love's shadows[4] are so rich in joy!

Enter Balthasar, booted

News from Verona! How now, Balthasar?
Dost thou not bring me letters from the friar?
How doth my lady? Is my father well?
How fares my Juliet? That I ask again;
For nothing can be ill if she be well.

Balthasar

Then she is well, and nothing can be ill;
Her body sleeps in Capel's monument,
And her immortal part with angels lives.
I saw her laid low in her kindred's vault,   20
And presently took post[5] to tell it you.
O! pardon me for bringing these ill news,
Since you did leave it for my office,[6] sir.

Romeo

Is it even so? then I defy you, stars!
Thou know'st my lodging: get me ink and paper,
And hire post-horses; I will hence to-night.

Balthasar

I do beseech you, sir, have patience:
Your looks are pale and wild, and do import[7]
Some misadventure.

[1]pleasant dreams
[2]foretell
[3]heart

[4]dreams of love

[5]came quickly

[6]business

[7]suggest

Romeo
                              Tush, thou art deceiv'd;
Leave me, and do the thing I bid thee do.   *30*
Hast thou no letters to me from the friar?

Balthasar
No, my good lord.

Romeo
                              No matter; get thee gone,
And hire those horses: I'll be with thee straight.

                                        [Exit Balthasar

Well, Juliet, I will lie with thee to-night.
Let's see for means: O mischief! thou art swift
To enter in the thoughts of desperate men.
I do remember an apothecary,[8]
And hereabouts he dwells, which late I noted
In tatter'd weeds,[9] with overwhelming brows,
Culling of simples;[10] meagre were his looks,   *40*
Sharp misery had worn him to the bones
And in his needy shop a tortoise hung,
An alligator stuff'd, and other skins
Of ill-shap'd fishes; and about his shelves
A beggarly account[11] of empty boxes,
Green earthen pots, bladders,[12] and musty seeds,
Remnants of packthread, and old cakes of roses,
Were thinly scatter'd, to make up a show.
Noting this penury,[13] to myself I said
An if a man did need a poison now,   *50*
Whose sale is present death in Mantua,
Here lives a caitiff[14] wretch would sell it him.
O! this same thought did but fore-run my need,
And this same needy man must sell it me.
As I remember, this should be the house:
Being holiday, the beggar's shop is shut.
What, ho! apothecary!

                              Enter Apothecary

Apothecary
                              Who calls so loud?

Romeo
Come hither, man. I see that thou art poor;
Hold, there is forty ducats;[15] let me have
A dram of poison, such soon-speeding gear[16]   *60*
As will disperse itself through all the veins
That the life-weary taker may fall dead,

[8]drug-dealer

[9]clothes

[10]picking plants

[11]number

[12]containers

[13]poverty

[14]miserable

[15]gold coins
[16]quick-acting poison

intents to take his
own life

And that the trunk may be discharg'd of breath
As violently as hasty powder fir'd
Ooth hurry from the fatal cannon's womb.

Apothecary

Such mortal drugs I have; but Mantua's law
Is death to any he that utters[17] them.   [17]sells

Romeo

Art thou so bare, and full of wretchedness,
And fear'st to die? famine is in thy cheeks,
Need and oppression starveth in thine eyes,   *70*
Contempt and beggary hang upon thy back;
The world is not thy friend nor the world's law:
The world affords no law to make thee rich;
Then be not poor, but break it, and take this.

Apothecary

My poverty, but not my will, consents.

Romeo

I pay thy poverty, and not thy will.

Apothecary

Put this in any liquid thing you will,
And drink it off; and, if you had the strength
Of twenty men, it would dispatch you straight.

Romeo

There is thy gold, worse poison to men's souls,   *80*
Doing more murders in this loathsome world
Than these poor compounds that thou mayst not
        sell:
I sell thee poison, thou hast sold me none.
Farewell; buy food, and get thyself in flesh.
Come, cordial[18] and not poison, go with me   [18]a restoring drink
To Juliet's grave, for there I must use thee.

                                    [Exeunt

Summary – Time: Later on Wednesday (or perhaps on Thursday)

Sad News for Romeo

Romeo, who left Juliet early on Tuesday morning, is now in exile in Mantua. Romeo relates a happy dream he has just had of being awakened by Juliet's kisses. He is expecting good news from the friar.

Balthasar rushes in with the shocking news that Juliet is dead. Sadly, Romeo prepares to leave for Verona, disappointed that he has received no message from Friar Laurence.

Balthasar leaves to get the horses. Romeo, left alone, decides that he will lie with Juliet in death that very night. Romeo goes to a poor apothecary who sells him a fast-acting poison in exchange for gold. Romeo intends to take the poison as a love potion to unite him with Juliet in her grave.

Scene Analysis

Romeo in Happy Mood

Romeo has had a joyful dream of being awakened from death by Juliet's kisses:

> "I dreamt my lady came and found me dead; —
> "...And breath'd such life with kisses in my lips,
> That I reviv'd, and was an emperor."

What Romeo anticipates is good news from Verona, but ironically he prophesies Juliet's awaking and finding him dead in the vault. He is not to be united with Juliet except in death.

Romeo Against the Odds

The news of Juliet's *"death"* arrives before Friar Laurence has informed Romeo of his plan. Romeo, believing that Juliet is really dead, is plunged into deep despair and decides to join her in death:

> "Well, Juliet, I will lie with thee to-night."

Fate has begun to close in on the *"star-cross'd"* lovers and has taken control of their destiny. Romeo knows only one answer to Fate and acquires poison from a poverty-stricken apothecary. Only one hope remains to save the lovers – that Juliet will awaken before Romeo dies. Will fate look kindly on the lovers at last?

However, Romeo does not intend to bow to the quirks of Fate: he will give his life for love and death will unite the lovers.

> "Come, cordial and not poison, go with me
> To Juliet's grave, for there I must use thee."

Our hearts go with him.

Characters

ROMEO

Romeo is no longer the impractical idealist he was before. He makes up his mind quickly and acts decisively. He has no time now for melancholy doubts, but springs into action calmly:

> *"Is it even so? then I defy you, stars!*
> *Thou know'st my lodging: get me ink and paper,*
> *And hire post-horses; I will hence to-night."*

Romeo becomes master of his own destiny in this scene. He courageously forms his desperate plan without hesitation and is determined to die to be united in love with Juliet. He attains the same heroic status that Juliet attained in *Act 4 Scene III*:

> *"Well, Juliet, I will lie with thee to-night,"* is as heroic as it is simple.

BALTHASAR

In this scene, Balthasar shows his loyalty to and concern for Romeo. He is as anxious as Romeo for good news and does not wish Romeo to act too hastily:

> *"I do beseech you, sir, have patience:*
> *Your looks are pale and wild, and do import*
> *Some misadventure."*

Scene II

Verona. Friar Laurence's Cell
Enter Friar John

Friar John
Holy Franciscan friar! brother, ho!

Enter Friar Laurence

Friar Laurence
This same should be the voice of Friar John.
Welcome from Mantua: what says Romeo?
Or, if his mind be writ, give me his letter.

Friar John
Going to find a bare-foot brother out,
One of our order, to associate[1] me,
Here in this city visiting the sick,
And finding him, the searchers[2] of the town,
Suspecting that we both were in a house

[1] accompany

[2] for the plague

153

[3]plague

Where the infectious pestilence[3] did reign,   10
Seal'd up the doors, and would not let us forth;
So that my speed to Mantua there was stay'd.
Friar Laurence
Who bear my letter then to Romeo?
Friar John
I could not send it, here it is again,
Nor get a messenger to bring it thee,
So fearful were they of infection.
Friar Laurence
Unhappy fortune! by my brotherhood,

[4]serious business
[5]great importance

The letter was not nice, but full of charge[4]
Of dear import;[5] and the neglecting it
May do much danger. Friar John, go hence;   20

[6]crow bar

Get me an iron crow,[6] and bring it straight
Unto my cell.
Friar John
          Brother, I'll go and bring it thee.   [Exit
Friar Laurence
Now must I to the monument alone;
Within these three hours will fair Juliet wake:

[7]blame
[8]events

She will beshrew[7] me much that Romeo
Hath had no notice of these accidents;[8]
But I will write again to Mantua,
And keep her at my cell till Romeo come:
Poor living corse, clos'd in a dead man's tomb!   [Exit

Summary – Time: Wednesday (or perhaps Thursday)

The Friar's Plan goes Wrong

Friar John calls to Friar Laurence's cell to explain why he could not deliver the message to Romeo about Friar Laurence's plan. Friar John was confined in a house suspected of plague and could get no one to take the letter for fear of infection.

Friar Laurence decides to go to the Capulet vault since he expects Juliet to awaken in three hours. He intends to hide Juliet in his cell until he can call Romeo from Mantua to be with her and thus hopes to prevent misfortune.

Scene Analysis

An Unfortunate Accident

In this scene we understand why Romeo has received no explanation from the friar of Juliet's pretended death – unfortunately the messenger was held up in a house suspected of plague and could not deliver the message. This unhappy accident leads to a race against time to prevent disaster. Romeo has already left Mantua and Juliet is about to awaken. The question uppermost in our minds is – can the friar be on time to prevent tragedy? We wait with bated breath, wondering if Romeo will kill himself before he finds out the true state of affairs. So many fateful accidents have already happened that we feel that disaster is imminent.

Characters

FRIAR LAURENCE

Friar Laurence acts decisively in this scene to prevent tragedy. He wishes to prevent *"much danger"* and shows his sympathy for Juliet enclosed in the vault:

> *"Poor living corse, clos'd in a dead man's tomb!"*

Scene III

*The Same. A Churchyard; in it a
Monument belonging to the Capulets*

Enter Paris, and his page, bearing flowers and a torch

Paris
Give me thy torch, boy: hence, and stand aloof;
Yet put it out, for I would not be seen.
Under yond yew-trees lay thee all along,
Holding thine ear close to the hollow ground:
So shall no foot upon the churchyard tread,
Being loose, unfirm with digging up of graves,
But thou shalt hear it: whistle then to me,
As signal that thou hear'st something approach.
Give me those flowers. Do as I bid thee; go.

Page *[Aside]*
I am almost afraid to stand alone   *10*
Here in the churchyard; yet I will adventure.¹   ¹dare

                                        [Retires

Paris

Sweet flower, with flowers thy bridal bed I strew,
O woe! thy canopy is dust and stones;
Which with sweet water nightly I will dew,
Or, wanting that, with tears distill'd by moans:
The obsequies² that I for thee will keep
Nightly shall be to strew thy grave and weep.

[The page whistles

The boy gives warning something doth approach.
What cursed foot wanders this way to-night,
To cross³ my obsequies and true love's rite?   20
What! with a torch? — muffle⁴ me, night, awhile.

[Retires

Enter Romeo and Balthasar, with a torch, mattock, etc.

Romeo

Give me that mattock,⁵ and the wrenching iron.
Hold, take this letter; early in the morning
See thou deliver it to my lord and father.
Give me the light: upon thy life I charge⁶ thee,
Whate'er thou hear'st or seest, stand all aloof,
And do not interrupt me in my course.⁷
Why I descend into this bed of death,
Is partly, to behold my lady's face;
But chiefly to take thence from her dead finger   30
A precious ring, a ring that I must use
In dear employment: therefore hence, be gone:
But, if thou, jealous,⁸ doth return to pry
In what I further shall intend to do,
By heaven, I will tear thee joint by joint,
And strew this hungry churchyard with thy limbs,
The time and my intents are savage-wild,
More fierce and more inexorable far
Than empty⁹ tigers or the roaring sea.

Balthasar

I will be gone, sir, and not trouble you.   40

Romeo

So shalt thou show me friendship. Take thou that:
Live, and be prosperous; and farewell, good
        fellow.

Balthasar *[Aside]*

For all this same, I'll hide me here about:
His looks I fear, and his intents I doubt.   *[Retires*

²funeral rites

³disturb
⁴hide

⁵pickaxe

⁶order

⁷business

⁸curious

⁹hungry

Romeo

Thou detestable maw,[10] thou womb of death,   [10]stomach
Gorg'd with the dearest morsel of the earth,
Thus I enforce thy rotten jaws to open,

[Opens the tomb

And, in despite, I'll cram thee with more food!

Paris

This is that banish'd haughty Montague,
That murder'd my love's cousin, with which grief   *50*
It is supposed the fair creature died;
And here is come to do some villanous shame
To the dead bodies: I will apprehend him. —

[Comes forward

Stop thy unhallow'd[11] toil, vile Montague,   [11]evil
Can vengeance be pursu'd further than death?
Condemned villain, I do apprehend thee:
Obey, and go with me; for thou must die.

Romeo

I must, indeed; and therefore came I hither.
Good gentle youth, tempt not a desperate man;
Fly hence and leave me: think upon these gone;   *60*
Let them affright thee. I beseech thee, youth,
Put not another sin upon my head
By urging me to fury: O! be gone:
By heaven, I love thee better than myself,
For I come hither arm'd against myself:
Stay not, be gone; live, and hereafter say
A madman's mercy bade thee run away.

Paris

I do defy thy conjurations,[12]   [12]advice
And apprehend thee for a felon[13] here.   [13]criminal

Romeo

Wilt thou provoke me? then have at thee, boy!   *70*

[They fight

Page

O Lord! they fight: I will go call the watch.   *[Exit*

Paris *[Falls]*

O, I am slain! — If thou be merciful,
Open the tomb, lay me with Juliet.   *[Dies]*

Romeo

In faith, I will. Let me peruse this face:

14confused, unlucky

Mercutio's kinsman, noble County Paris!
What said my man when my betossed[14] soul
Did not attend him as we rode? I think
He told me Paris should have married Juliet:
Said he not so? or did I dream it so?
Or am I mad, hearing him talk of Juliet,   80
To think it was so? O! give me thy hand,
One writ with me in sour misfortune's book:
I'll bury thee in a triumphant grave;
A grave? O, no! a lanthom, slaughter'd youth,
For here lies Juliet, and her beauty makes
This vault a feasting presence full of light.

15buried

Death, lie thou there, by a dead man interr'd,[15]

                                    [Laying Paris in the tomb

How oft when men are at the point of death
Have they been merry! which their keepers call

16a burst of good spirits

A lightning[16] before death: O! how may I   90
Call this a lightning? O my love! my wife!
Death, that hath suck'd the honey of thy breath,
Hath had no power yet upon thy beauty:

17banner, flag

Thou art not conquer'd; beauty's ensign[17] yet
Is crimson in thy lips and in thy cheeks,
And death's pale flag is not advanced there.
Tybalt, liest thou there in thy bloody sheet?
O! what more favour can I do thee,
Than with that hand that cut thy youth in twain

18separate

To sunder[18] his that was thine enemy?   100
Forgive me, cousin! Ah! dear Juliet,
Why art thou yet so fair? Shall I believe
That unsubstantial Death is amorous,
And that the lean abhorred monster keeps

19lover

Thee here in dark to be his paramour?[19]
For fear of that I still will stay with thee,
And never from this palace of dim night
Depart again: here, here will I remain
With worms that are thy chambermaids; O! here
Will I set up my everlasting rest,   110

20unfavourable

And shake the yoke of inauspicious[20] stars
From this world-wearied flesh. Eyes, look your last!
Arms, take your last embrace! and, lips, O you
The doors of breath, seal with a righteous kiss

21everlasting

A dateless[21] bargain to engrossing death!
Come, bitter conduct, come, unsavoury guide!

22Romeo himself

Thou desperate pilot,[22] now at once run on
The dashing rocks thy sea-sick weary bark!

Here's to my love! *[Drinks]* O true apothecary!
Thy drugs are quick. Thus with a kiss I die.   *120 [Dies*

*Enter, at the other end of the Churchyard, Friar Laurence,
with a lanthorn, crow, and space*

Friar Laurence

Saint Francis be my speed! how oft to-night
Have my old feet stumbled at graves! Who's there?

Balthasar

Here's one, a friend, and one that knows you well.

Friar Laurence

Bliss be upon you! Tell me, good my friend,
What torch is yond, that vainly²³ lends his light   ²³in vain
To grubs and eyeless skulls? as I discern,
It burneth in the Capel's monument.

Balthasar

It doth so, holy sir; and there's my master,
One that you love.

Friar Laurence

    Who is it?

Balthasar

      Romeo.

Friar Laurence

How long hath he been there?

Balthasar

      Full half an hour.   *130*

Friar Laurence

Go with me to the vault.

Balthasar

    I dare not, sir.
My master knows not but I am gone hence;
And fearfully did menace me with death
If I did stay to look on his intents.

Friar Laurence

Stay then, I'll go alone. Fear comes upon me;
O! much I fear some ill unthrifty thing.

Balthasar

As I did sleep under this yew-tree here,
I dreamt my master and another fought,
And that my master slew him.

Friar Laurence [Advances]

        Romeo!

Alack, alack! what blood is this which stains   140
The stony entrance of this sepulchre?

²⁴abandoned

What mean these masterless²⁴ and gory swords
To lie discolour'd by this place of peace?

                                      [Enters the tomb

Romeo! O, pale! Who else? what! Paris too?
And steep'd in blood? Ah! what an unkind hour
Is guilty of this lamentable chance.
The lady stirs.   [Juliet wakes

Juliet

O, comfortable friar! where is my lord?
I do remember well where I should be,
And there I am. Where is my Romeo?   150

                                      [Noise within

Friar Laurence

I hear some noise, Lady, come from that nest

²⁵disease

Of death, contagion,²⁵ and unnatural sleep:
A greater power than we can contradict
Hath thwarted our intents: come, come away.
Thy husband in thy bosom there lies dead;
And Paris too: come, I'll dispose of thee
Among a sisterhood of holy nuns.
Stay not to question, for the watch is coming;
Come, go, good Juliet. — [Noise again] I dare no
      longer stay.

Juliet

Go, get thee hence, for I will not away.   160

                                  [Exit Friar Laurence

What's here? a cup, clos'd in my true love's hand?
Poison, I see, hath been his timeless end.

²⁶fool

O churl!²⁶ drunk all, and left no friendly drop
To help me after! I will kiss thy lips;
Haply; some poison yet doth hang on them,
To make me die with a restorative.   [Kisses him
Thy lips are warm!

First Watch. [Within]

Lead, boy: which way?

Juliet

Yea, noise? then I'll be brief. O happy dagger!

                                  [Snatching Romeo's dagger

This is thy sheath; *[Stabs herself]* there rust, and   *170*
    let me die.
[Falls on Romeo's body and dies

Enter Watch, with the Page of Paris

Page
This is the place; there where the torch doth burn.

First Watch
The ground[27] is bloody; search about the churchyard.   [27]cause
Go, some of you; who'er you find, attach.
[Exeunt some of the Watch

Pitiful sight! here lies the county slain,
And Juliet bleeding, warm, and newly dead,
Who here hath lain these two days buried.
Go, tell the prince, run to the Capulets,
Raise up the Montagues, some others search:
[Exeunt others of the Watch

We see the ground whereon these woes do lie;
But the true ground of all these piteous woes   *180*
We cannot without circumstance descry.[28]   [28]discover

Re-enter some of the Watch, with Balthasar

Second Watch
Here's Romeo's man; we found him in the churchyard.

First Watch
Hold him in safety, till the prince come hither.

Re-enter other of the Watch, with Friar Laurence

Third Watch
Here is a friar, that trembles, sighs, and weeps;
We took this mattock and this spade from him,
As he was coming from this churchyard side.

First Watch
A great suspicion; stay the friar too.

Enter the Prince and Attendants

Prince
What misadventure is so early up,
That calls our person from our morning rest?

Enter Capulet, Lady Capulet and Others

Capulet

What should it be, that they so shriek abroad?   *190*

Lady Capulet

The people in the street cry Romeo,
Some Juliet, and some Paris; and all run
With open outcry toward our monument.

Prince

What fear is this which startles in our ears?

First Watch

Sovereign, here lies the County Paris slain;
And Romeo dead; and Juliet, dead before,
Warm and new kill'd.

Prince

Search, seek, and know how this foul murder
        comes.

First Watch

Here is a friar, and slaughter'd Romeo's man;
With instruments[29] upon them, fit to open   *200*
These dead men's tombs.

Capulet

O, heaven! — O wife! look how our daughter
        bleeds!
This dagger hath mista'en![30] — for, lo, his
        house[31]
Is empty on the back of Montague
And is mis-sheathed in my daughter's bosom.

Lady Capulet

O me! this sight of death is as a bell,
That warns[32] myoid age to a sepulchre.

                    Enter Montague and Others

Prince

Come, Montague: for thou art early up,
To see thy son and heir more early down.

Montague

Alas! my liege, my wife is dead to-night;   *210*
Grief of my son's exile hath stopp'd her breath.
What further woe conspires[33] against mine age?

Prince

Look, and thou shalt see.

Montague

O thou untaught![34] what manners is in this,

---

[29]tools

[30]made a mistake
[31]sheath

[32]summons

[33]plots

[34]ill-mannered

To press[35] before thy father to a grave?

Prince

Seal up the mouth of outrage for a while,
Till we can clear these ambiguities, → *unclear*
And know their spring,[36] their head, their true
    descent;
And then will I be general[37] of your woes,
And lead you even to death: meantime forbear,
And let mischance be slave to[38] patience.
Bring forth the parties of suspicion.

Friar Laurence

I am the greatest, able to do least,
Yet most suspected, as the time and place
Doth make against me, of this direful[39] murder;
And here I stand, both to impeach[40] and purge[41]
Myself condemned and myself excus'd.

Prince

Then say at once what thou dost know in[42] this.

Friar Laurence

I will be brief, for my short date of breath[43]
Is not so long as is a tedious tale.
Romeo, there dead, was husband to that Juliet;
And she, there dead, that Romeo's faithful wife:
I married them; and their stolen[44] marriage-day
Was Tybalt's doomsday, whose untimely death
Banish'd the new-made bridegroom from this city;
For whom, and not for Tybalt, Juliet pin'd.
You, to remove that siege of grief from her,
Betroth'd,[45] and would have married her
    perforce,[46]
To County Paris: then comes she to me,
And, with wild looks bid me devise some mean[47]
To rid her from this second marriage,
Or in my cell there would she kill herself.
Then gave I her,— so tutor'd by my art, —
A sleeping potion; which so took effect
As I intended, for it wrought on her
The form[48] of death: meantime I writ to Romeo
That he should hither come as[49] this dire night,
To help to take her from her borrow'd grave,
Being the time the potion's force should cease,
But he which bore my letter, Friar John,
Was stay'd by accident, and yesternight
Return'd my letter back. Then, all alone,

220

230

240

250

[35]rush

[36]cause

[37]leader

[38]be subject to

[39]dreadful
[40]accuse
[41]defend

[42]about

[43]life

[44]secret

[45]pledged in marriage
[46]by force

[47]method

[48]appearance
[49]on

At the prefixed hour of her waking,
Came I to take her from her kindred's vault,
Meaning to keep her closely at my cell,
Till I conveniently could send to Romeo:
But, when I came, — some minute ere the time
Of her awakening, — here untimely lay
The noble Paris and true Romeo dead.
She wakes; and I entreated her come forth,   260
And bear this work of heaven with patience;
But then a noise did scare me from the tomb,
And she, too desperate, would not go with me,
But, as it seems, did violence on herself.
All this I know; and to the marriage
Her nurse is privy:⁵⁰ and, if aught in this
Miscarried by my fault, let my old life
Be sacrific'd, some hour before his⁵¹ time,
Unto the rigour of severest law.

Prince

We still have known thee for a holy man.   270
Where's Romeo's man? what can he say to this?

Balthasar

I brought my master news of Juliet's death;
And then in post⁵² he came from Mantua
To this same place, to this same monument.
This letter he early bid me give his father,
And threaten'd me with death, going in the vault,
If I departed not and left him there.

Prince

Give me the letter; I will look on it.
Where is the county's page that rais'd the watch?
Sirrah, what made your master⁵³ in this place?   280

Page

He came with flowers to strew his lady's grave,
And bid me stand aloof, and so I did;
Anon, comes one with light to ope the tomb;
And by and by my master drew on him;
And then I ran away to call the watch.

Prince

This letter doth make good⁵⁴ the friar's words,
Their course of love, the tidings of her death:
And here he writes that he did buy a poison
Of a poor 'pothecary, and therewithal⁵⁵
Came to this vault to die, and lie with Juliet.   290

⁵⁰knows

⁵¹its

⁵²very quickly

⁵³what was your master doing?

⁵⁴confirm

⁵⁵with that

Where be these enemies? — Capulet! Montague!
See what a scourge is laid upon your hate,
That heaven finds means to kill your joys with love;
And I, for winking at your discords too,
Have lost a brace[56] of kinsmen: all are punish'd.

Capulet

O brother Montague! give me thy hand:
This is my daughter's jointure,[57] for no more
Can I demand.

Montague

          But I can give thee more;
For I will raise her statue in pure gold;
That while Verona by that name is known,   *300*
There shall no figure at such rate[58] be set
As that of true and faithful Juliet.

Capulet

As rich shall Romeo's by his lady's lie;
Poor sacrifices of our enmity!

Prince

A glooming[59] peace this morning with it brings;
The sun, for sorrow, will not show his head:
Go hence, to have more talk of these sad things:
Some shall be pardon'd, and some punished:
For never was a story of more woe
Than this of Juliet and her Romeo.   *310*
                                                  [Exeunt

[56]two

[57]marriage settlement from her husband (opposite to a dowry)

[58]high value

[59]dark, sad

Summary – Time: Wednesday night to Thursday morning (or perhaps a day later)

Paris and Romeo at the Vault

In the Capulet vault at night, Paris grieves for his lost bride in a mourning ceremony and scatters flowers on the ground. He is interrupted by Romeo who is trying to break into the vault to be with Juliet in death.

Paris thinks that Romeo has come to dishonour the Capulet tomb and tries to arrest him as a double felon. Romeo and Paris fight and Paris is killed. Romeo recognises Paris and regrets killing him. He drags Paris's body into the tomb and lays it beside Juliet.

The Deaths of the Lovers

Alone, Romeo meditates on Juliet's beauty as she lies in the tomb, life-like in her wedding clothes. Looking at the dead Tybalt, Romeo asks his forgiveness for killing him. Romeo then calls on Death to unite him with his love, takes the poison and dies, with a last kiss to Juliet's lips.

Just then Friar Laurence and Balthasar enter at the other end of the churchyard. The friar is horrified to find both Romeo and Paris dead and blames Fate for this disaster.

At this moment, Juliet awakens calmly and asks for Romeo. Friar Laurence tells her Romeo is dead and he leaves quickly to avoid the appoaching townspeople.

Juliet refuses to leave with him. Finding Romeo poisoned, Juliet stabs herself with his dagger and lovingly falls dead on his body.

Love Overcomes Hate

The watchmen find the pitiful sight in the vault and search the churchyard. Balthasar and Friar Laurence are arrested. The Prince is sent for and arrives with the Capulets. All are dumbfounded. Montague arrives, without his wife, who has died from grief for Romeo's exile. He too is shocked at the loss of his son.

The Prince then tries to sort out the disaster. Friar Laurence then relates the whole story, blaming the disaster on fate but accepting blame for his part in the sad events. Balthasar, with Romeo's letter, and Paris's page confirm the truth of the friar's account.

The Prince then gives his judgment and places the main blame for the tragedy on the feuding families of Verona, who kept up their hostilities so long. He blames himself for his failure to take firmer action to stop the feud.

Both families purge their guilt and agree to be reconciled. Each will erect a golden statue of the other's child as a reminder to all of how love overcame hate through the death of the lovers.

Scene Analysis

A Sense of Impending Doom

Skilfully Shakespeare sets the scene for the tragic events in this scene. The atmosphere of the churchyard is eerie and full of fear. It is dark and the flickering torches and lanterns lend an unearthly aura to the scene. The page is afraid to be alone in the silence and darkness among the graves. The sounds of crow-bars and mattocks wrenching, warning whistles and shuffling feet intensify the atmosphere of terror and heighten the effects of the violent deaths of the lovers on a sympathetic audience.

Ah! dear Juliet,
Why art thou yet so fair? Shall I believe
That unsubstantial Death is amorous,
And that the lean abhorred monster keeps
Thee here in dark to be his paramour?

(Romeo, Act 5, Scene III)

The Tragic Forces Close In

The tragic deaths of Romeo and Juliet come about by a series of unfortunate accidents which come to a head in this scene.

(i)   Romeo has not been told that Juliet is not really dead, since the friar's letter failed to reach him.

(ii) Friar Laurence arrives too late at the vault to prevent Romeo's sacrifice to love.

(iii) Juliet awakens too late to save Romeo's life.

(iv) Friar Laurence is too slow to realise that Juliet intends to die with her lover and he escapes without her.

(v)   The watchmen, summoned by the page, arrive too late to prevent the deaths.

Had these accidental events not happened, the tragedy might have been averted. It is as if fate or bad luck ordained this tragedy.

In the wider context of the world of Verona, it is not just Fate or accident that we blame for the tragedy. It is the long-standing hatred of the feud between the families and the repeated misunderstandings and prejudices of the friends and families of the lovers that are the real causes of the catastrophe. When the lovers were faced with great problems to solve, they found themselves isolated and deserted by those who might have helped them. More tragic than the accidents that might not have happened (perhaps in a better society) is the reality that society itself has driven its children to their untimely deaths. Thus, in this scene, society and Fate combine to cause the tragedy:

> *"See what a scourge is laid upon your hate,*
> *That heaven finds means to kill your joys with love;"*

The Power of Love

The play does not end in total despair. It presents a new beginning, a new understanding, and we look forward to better things in the future. The lovers' sacrifice has not been in vain since the Capulets and the Montagues both come to their senses and are reconciled. Too bad that it needed the deaths of their children to bring peace and understanding to Verona:

> *"A glooming peace this morning with it brings;*
> *The sun, for sorrow, will not show his head:"*

For the lovers themselves, their love brings victory over Fate and hatred and even over death itself. In death, the lovers are together and, in a sense, "live happily ever after", since their love transcends death:

> *"...O! here*
> *Will I set up my everlasting rest,*
> *And shake the yoke of inauspicious stars*
> *From this world-wearied flesh."*

In a sense, the *"star-cross'd"* lovers have themselves become stars to beam down love from heaven to redeem Verona.

> *"heaven finds means to kill your joys with love."*

Characters

ROMEO

Romeo is a tragic hero in this scene. He realises there is no turning back from his purpose and he faces death without flinching:

> *"Here's to my love!...*
> *...Thus with a kiss I die."*

His death is not an act of despair but an act of pure love. He looks forward to togetherness with Juliet in death and this outweighs the desperation of his actions:

> *"...here lies Juliet, and her beauty makes*
> *This vault a feasting presence full of light."*

> *"For fear of that I will stay with thee,"*

JULIET

Juliet's death shows heroic courage in stabbing herself with a dagger, a more painful death than poison. Yet she does not hesitate despite the violence required:

> *"Yea, noise? then I'll be brief O happy dagger!*
> *This is thy sheath; there rust, and let me die."*

She needed no rationalisation to drive her to follow Romeo.

PARIS

Paris redeems himself in this scene by his bravery and secret devotion to Juliet. He dies defending the honour of the Capulets, which he thinks Romeo wishes to defile. He wished only the best to Juliet and is not to blame for the tragedy. He believes Romeo caused her death through grief for Tybalt:

> *"I do defy thy conjurations,*
> *And apprehend thee for a felon here."*

> *"Open the tomb, lay me with Juliet."*

CAPULET AND MONTAGUE

Capulet is the first to offer to end the hostilities. He genuinely regrets his part in the untimely deaths of Romeo and Juliet:

> *"O brother Montague! give me thy hand:"*

A contrast to his earlier extravagance!

Montague is also chastened by the tragic events. He wishes to honour Juliet above all others by a golden statue, towering higher than any other in Verona.

THE PRINCE

As always the Prince sorts out the problems and tempers justice with mercy. He admits his own blame in not being firmer in stopping the feud:

> *"Some shall be pardon'd, and some punished:"*

FRIAR LAURENCE

Friar Laurence arrives too late to save Romeo. When Juliet awakens she asks for Romeo, but the friar insensitively and abruptly tells her he is dead. Conscious of his own reputation and safety, he deserts Juliet when she most needs him.

> *"I dare no longer stay."*

He is unable to cope, despite his former moralising. He contrasts with the steadfast Juliet who says to him:

> *"Go, get thee hence, for I will not away."*

Part 3
FURTHER STUDY

Tragedy

Is *Romeo and Juliet* really a Tragedy?

Romeo and Juliet is usually included among Shakespeare's tragedies, but Shakespeare wrote this play in 1595, long before his "great" tragedies, *Hamlet*, *Othello*, *King Lear* and *Macbeth*. It differs in many fundamental elements from these later tragedies, but is nonetheless a tragedy despite the differences.

In the later tragedies, a single hero of outstanding character and status undertakes an important course of action which, in the end, brings him great misfortune and death, because of some weakness or extreme element in his own character. In *Romeo and Juliet*, a hero and a heroine, who are little more than children, simply fall in love in an unsympathetic society and suffer death as a result of a number of random and accidental circumstances or coincidences. It would be correct to conclude that *Romeo and Juliet* is not a tragedy in the purest sense of the word (as defined by Aristotle and A.C. Bradley). However, it would be a serious mistake to suggest that *Romeo and Juliet* is not really a tragedy at all. It is a tragedy, and a "great" one at that, but a tragedy of a different kind. As a tragedy, *Romeo and Juliet* has much in common with modern tragedy (whether *West Side Story* or the plays of Eugene O'Neill), in which society, and not any "tragic flaw" in the hero's character or judgement, is mainly responsible for the catastrophe that befalls the hero.

What is Tragedy?

Tragedy, since the time of Aristotle and the Greek tragedies of Sophocles and Euripides, has continued to evolve over the years. Many attempts have been made to find a definition that can include both the great classical tragedies and the more down-to-earth modern tragedies. There is, however, no such all-embracing definition, and the best we can do is to suggest the main characteristics of what we recognise as tragedy.

(a) The tragic hero or heroine should command our earnest goodwill. He does not need to be a superman but should command our respect so that we can identify with him in the course of action he undertakes.

(b) The hero should undertake a serious course of action which will, through a series of actions, lead directly to some grave misfortune or catastrophe. Usually the hero will have some flaw in character or judgement that will help to bring about the catastrophe.

(c) In the world in which the tragic action is undertaken by the hero, it must be credible that the action undertaken should lead with some sense of inevitability to the misfortunes or catastrophe. Accidental misfortunes do not make great tragedies.

(d) As the hero tries to cope with the adverse circumstances or problems he meets, he should be confronted with further reversals of fortune, which stack the odds against him even higher, making his attempts to escape misfortune even more ineffective the more he tries.

(e) While the hero need not necessarily cause his catastrophe through some tragic flaw in his character or judgement, he must at least recognise that he is somehow caught on a path to unavoidable misfortune or catastrophe. Ideally he should also recognise his own role in bringing about this catastrophe.

(f) A tragedy should arouse tragic emotions of pity and fear in the audience. Usually this will come about because the extent of the catastrophe will be out of proportion to what the hero's actions deserve.

Briefly then, in a tragedy a hero, whom we respect, undertakes a course of action which leads inevitably to catastrophe, through a credible sequence of events, involving reversals of fortune and recognition of his situation, and the audience experiences tragic emotions of pity and fear which are refined with a note of hope for the future.

Romeo and Juliet as a Tragedy

Romeo and Juliet displays many of the characteristics of tragedy mentioned above.

(a) Romeo and Juliet seldom fail to gain our sympathy and understanding. Because of their youth, sincerity and courage, we identify closely with them as their attempts to fulfil their love for each other isolate them from a hostile and unsympathetic society and part them from each other as they begin their married life. As they struggle to find happiness in a world of hate, we hope against hope that they will succeed. In their struggle to survive, they each display heroic qualitites of courage and self-sacrifice and merit our admiration and sympathy.

(b) It is the lovers' determination to remain faithful to each other, despite the hostile and unloving world of Verona, which leads to their deaths. They died because they loved in a world of hate. Catastrophe could have been avoided if they had not fallen in love or if their idealistic love had bowed to the demands of the unsympathetic society of Verona.

(c) It is credible that hate and evil should destroy love, whenever hate is in control. The corruption of society by hate and evil makes it inevitable that Romeo and Juliet should suffer grave misfortune. In such a society, accidents (such as the killing of Tybalt, the friar's delayed letter, Romeo arriving too soon at the Capulet vault and poisoning himself) are perhaps more likely to happen than in a normal world and when they do happen, can have more devastating consequences. In such a society, the hero and the heroine are driven to hasty, even impetuous actions (the hasty killing of Tybalt by Romeo, the hasty marriage, the hasty plan to prevent Juliet's marriage to Paris and the hasty suicides). The heroes' haste and the hostility of society both contribute to bringing misfortune and death, but it is society that is the main cause of tragedy in *Romeo and Juliet*. The accidents and coincidences in the play do not take from the overall tragic effect of the play, but serve to intensify the sense of waste which dominates the end of the play. Thus *Romeo and Juliet* is unusual among Shakespeare's tragedies since the "tragic flaw" is more in society than in the heroes themselves.

(d) Both Romeo and Juliet take desperate steps to avert misfortune. Juliet agrees to Friar Laurence's plan to put her to sleep to avoid a bigamous marriage to Paris. Romeo buys poison when he hears of Juliet's death, in order to be with Juliet in death. Both of these remedies, far from improving the situation, lead directly to the deaths of the lovers. But for the hasty arrangement of Juliet's marriage to Paris (*"reversal"*) and the failure to inform Romeo of the friar's plan, catastrophe might have been avoided and the friar would have had an opportunity to persuade the hostile families to accept Romeo and Juliet's marriage. But time is not favourable to the lovers and its swiftness brings tragedy.

(e) Both Romeo and Juliet have premonitions of disaster. Juliet recognises that she is caught in a dilemma when she hears that her wedding to Paris is to take place a day earlier than planned. As she takes the potion she realises she is confronting her destiny. When Romeo hears of Juliet's "death", he realises there is no turning back from his fate and he buys poison. Juliet, when she awakens to discover Romeo dead, sees that she has no choice but to die with him. Thus there are many examples of "recognition" in the play.

(f) *Romeo and Juliet* leaves the audience with a tremendous sense of the waste of young love. The audience is sad that the lovers have to die to be together in love and to bring the society of Verona to its senses. However, as in most tragedies of Shakespeare, catharsis or uplifting of emotions takes place at the end of the tragedy. We are glad that the lovers did not die in vain, since their sacrifice brought reconciliation and peace to their families and to Verona. Order is restored and we hope for a new beginning.

Structure

The Structure of the Tragedy

Romeo and Juliet falls naturally into five divisions.

1. The Exposition: Act 1 Scenes I–IV

This section provides us with information about the world of Verona and the main characters in the drama and points us towards events which will follow.

The Prologue prepares us for a tragedy of love, involving Romeo and Juliet, which causes the lovers' deaths because of the hatred in Verona.

Act 1 Scene I	shows us first-hand the feuding and hostility in Verona and Romeo in love with love.
Act 1 Scene III	introduces us to Juliet's world of innocence and leads us to believe she will marry Paris.
Act 1 Scene IV	displays Mercutio's wit and gaiety and Romeo's premonitions of disaster to follow their attendance at Capulet's feast.

2. The Complication: Act 1 Scene V–Act 2 Scene VI

In this section, the plot thickens and events begin to rise. We learn more of the characters already introduced.

Act 1 Scene V	reminds us again of the feud by introducing Tybalt. Romeo and Juliet fall in love at Capulet's feast and begin their mission of love.
Act 2 Scene I	The Prologue suggests that love will overcome danger. Romeo escapes from his friends, seeking his new-found love.
Act 2 Scene II	shows us at once a moment of true happiness in love for Romeo and Juliet and a moment of absolute isolation from the hate-ridden society of Verona.
Act 2 Scene III	shows Romeo arranging with Friar Laurence to marry Juliet in secret.
Act 2 Scene IV	tells of Tybalt's challenge to Romeo and shows us a new Romeo full of life and love as he plans his marriage, with the nurse's help as messenger, to Juliet.
Act 2 Scene V	shows a tense and eager Juliet awaiting the news of her marriage plans from the teasing nurse.
Act 2 Scene VI	shows the two lovers very much in love and ready to fight against all obstacles to fulfil their love.

3. The Climax or Crisis: Act 3 Scene I

This is the turning point of the drama. The opposing forces have begun their progress and suspense is greatest in this scene. The challenge of Tybalt bears fruit and Mercutio is killed. Romeo is drawn into the web of violence and hatred, kills Tybalt and is banished on his wedding day. All seems spoiled for the lovers and tragedy begins.

4. The Resolution: Act 3 Scene II–Act 5 Scene II

The happiness of the lovers gradually becomes more and more remote as the obstacles begin to surround them.

Act 3 Scene II	is a scene of contrast which begins with Juliet, an eager bride, awaiting her husband and ends with the tragic news of his banishment from Verona.
Act 3 Scene III	shows Romeo in dire straits since he is banished, a fate worse than death for him. Friar Laurence attempts to advise and console him and promises to sort out the problem while Romeo is in Mantua.
Act 3 Scene IV	shows Capulet enthusiastically arranging Juliet's marriage to Paris for the following Thursday. At this time Romeo and Juliet spend their wedding night together.
Act 3 Scene V	shows the lovers' sad farewell and Juliet isolated but courageous. The forces of hate begin to close in on the lovers.
Act 4 Scene I	shows us Friar Laurence's desperate plan to save Juliet from a marriage to Paris. He is to send a message to Romeo.
Act 4 Scene II	shows Juliet isolated from her family as her father changes the wedding date to Wednesday.
Act 4 Scene III	shows Juliet heroically sacrificing herself for love as she risks death by taking the friar's potion.
Act 4 Scene IV	shows the happy Capulet household boisterously preparing for the wedding feast. It is a brief moment of relief from the tragedy that is now at hand.
Act 4 Scene V	is a scene of grief as Juliet is found "dead".
Act 5 Scene I	shows Romeo confronting the sad news of Juliet's "death" and making plans to die by her side.
Act 5 Scene II	shows how the friar's plan begins to go wrong, since the letter to Romeo has not been sent.

5. The Catastrophe: Act 5 Scene III

In this section the plot gathers to a conclusion and the action of the play is completed.

Romeo arrives at the vault before Juliet awakens and poisons himself to be with her in death. Juliet awakens and stabs herself to be united in love with Romeo. The families are reconciled and the sacrifice of the lovers leads to peace and harmony in Verona.

Themes

The Themes of the Play

A. Love and Hate
B. The "Generation Gap"
C. What is Love?
D. Feud, Fate and Flaw

A. Love and Hate

The central theme of *Romeo and Juliet* is a love which overcomes hate. It is a story of *"A pair of star-cross'd lovers"* who *"with their death bury their parents' strife"*. Romeo and Juliet fall in love in a world of feuding and hostility, but their steadfast love for each other struggles against all obstacles and in the end brings love and reconciliation to Verona.

In *Act 1 Scene I* we see the extent of the hatred in the society of Verona as the play opens with a battle on Verona's streets. All are involved in disturbing the peace of Verona, from the servants, to the young men and even to the rival family heads. Prince Excalus tries in vain to solve the problem, saying:

> *"If ever you disturb our streets again*
> *Your lives shall pay the forfeit of the peace."*

In *Act 3 Scene I* the Prince tries yet again to quell the violence on the streets of Verona which led to the deaths of Mercutio and Tybalt.

> *"I will be deaf to pleading and excuses;*
> *Nor tears nor prayers shall purchase out abuses;*
> *Therefore use none; let Romeo hence in haste,*
> *Else, when he's found, that hour is his last.*
> *Bear hence this body and attend our will:*
> *Mercy but murders, pardoning those that kill."*

However, all the Prince's efforts fail to restore peace to Verona.

After the slaying of Tybalt, Lady Capulet seeks vengeance for his death, even though it was Tybalt who caused his own death by seeking to punish Romeo for daring to attend Capulet's feast:

> *"I beg for justice, which thou, prince, must give;*
> *Romeo slew Tybalt, Romeo must not live."*

The same Tybalt in *Act 1 Scene I* shows his utter contempt for peace:

> *"What! drawn, and talk of peace? I hate the word,*
> *As I hate hell, all Montagues, and thee."*

Thus we see that hatred and vengeance are rife in Verona and even the Prince cannot bring peace. Benvolio's efforts to bring peace were also in vain when he failed to persuade Mercutio to stay off the streets:

> *"I pray the good Mercutio, let's retire:*
> *The day is hot, the Capulets abroad,*
> *And if we meet, we shall not 'scape a brawl;*
> *For now, these hot days, is the mad blood stirring."*

Friar Laurence's efforts to restore peace to Verona are also a failure and all he can do is adopt a desperate and ill-fated plan to save the lovers.

The love of Romeo and Juliet brings a new ray of hope to strife-torn Verona in *Act 2 Scene II*, as the lovers declare their true love for each other which transcends the hatred of their families. Romeo declares:

> *"I am no pilot; yet, wert thou as far*
> *As that vast shore wash'd with the*
> *furthest sea,*
> *I would adventure for such merchandise."*

Juliet declares that her love is more important than all else, saying:

> *"O Romeo, Romeo! wherefore art thou Romeo?*
> *Deny thy father and refuse thy name;*
> *Or if thou wilt not, be but sworn my love,*
> *And I'll no longer be a Capulet."*

Thus the lovers take on the hatred of the world, hoping to transform it into love.

As they try to overcome society's obstacles to their love later on in the play, they each sacrifice all for the sake of love. In *Act 3 Scene V*, Juliet puts Romeo's safety before her own desire to keep him with her in Verona:

> *"It is, it is [morning]: hie hence, be gone, away!"*

In *Act 4 Scene III*, Juliet is confronted with a marriage to Paris, a day earlier than she had anticipated, but she does not hesitate to risk even death itself by taking the friar's potion. She takes on the hatred and misunderstanding of her family and friends in this scene for the sake of her love for Romeo:

> *"Romeo, I come! this do I drink to thee."*

Confronted with the report of Juliet's "death" in *Act 5 Scene I*, Romeo too prepares to sacrifice himself for love, saying:

> *"Well, Juliet, I will lie with thee to-night."*

The sacrifices of the lovers culminate in the tragic suicides of the lovers in *Act 5 Scene III* when they both decide to die rather than be separated by a hostile world. All seems lost.

But just a little later in the scene, love triumphs over death and hatred, as the grief-stricken families and all of Verona lament the untimely deaths of their children. Where all else had failed to bring peace and harmony to Verona, the young lovers, by their example and sacrifices, reconciled their families and brought a much-needed peace to Verona. Love overcame hatred and the lovers' deaths were not in vain:

> *"A glooming peace this morning with it brings;*
> *The sun, for sorrow, will not show his head:"*

Order is restored in the disordered world of Verona and normal life may proceed.

B. The Generation Gap

Another theme in *Romeo and Juliet* is the "generation gap"; the tragic failure of parents and children to understand each other and make allowance for each other's needs. The lovers, as a consequence of this "generation gap", are isolated from their families and friends and must confront their problems alone.

Juliet's father, Old Capulet, said he would allow Juliet to choose her husband, but yet he arranges for her to marry Paris without asking her first. He is angry when she refuses to do what he says and disowns her heartlessly in *Act 3 Scene V*:

> *"An you be mine, I'll give you to my friend;*
> *An you be not, hang, beg, starve, die in the streets,*
> *For, by my soul, I'll ne'er acknowledge thee,"*

Juliet's mother has little sympathy or understanding for her daughter and coldly dismisses her:

> *"Talk not to me, for I'll not speak a word.*
> *Do as thou wilt, for I have done with thee."*

The nurse too lets Juliet down and Juliet loses a confidante since she will not betray Romeo by pretending to marry Paris. Juliet says to the nurse:

> *"...Go counsellor;*
> *Thou and my bosom henceforth shall be twain.*
> *I'll to the friar, to know his remedy:*
> *If all else fail, myself have power to die."*

Romeo's friends fail to understand his true love for Juliet and are more interested in teasing him. Mercutio sees his attitude to Tybalt as cowardice in *Act 3 Scene I* when Romeo tries to make peace with Tybalt who is cousin of Juliet.

> *"O calm, dishonourable, vile submission!"*

When Romeo turns to Friar Laurence for help, the friar tries his best but can only preach morality to Romeo. Romeo realises that the friar's advice is of little help and rejects it in *Act 3 Scene III*:

> *"Thou canst not speak of that thou dost not feel:*
> *Wert thou as young as I, Juliet thy love,*
> *An hour but married, Tybalt murdered,*
> *Doting like me, and like me banished,*
> *Then mightst thou speak, then mightst thou tear thy hair,*
> *And fall upon the ground, as I do now,"*

Thus Romeo and Juliet are isolated and have no one to help or understand them. It is this "generation gap" which makes the tragedy so intense, since it is those closest to the hero and heroine who fail them in their time of greatest need.

C. What is Love?

Throughout *Romeo and Juliet*, Shakespeare portrays many aspects of love and, in a sense, the play attempts to define what love is. Various characters exemplify and portray to us different kinds of love and the true love of Romeo and Juliet for each other is examined in the context of other views of love.

(a) Physical Pleasure and Lust

In the opening scene of the play, *Act 1 Scene I*, Sampson and Gregory, the Capulet servants, show us a bawdy, physical and sexual view of love. For them, love is lust finding its fulfilment in exploiting women for man's physical pleasure. Sampson says:

> *"...when I*
> *have fought with the men, I will be cruel with the*
> *maids; I will cut off their heads."*

and

> *":therefore women, being the weaker*
> *vessels, are ever thrust to the wall:"*

For the nurse, love is physical and sexual, for pleasure and pregnancy. She enjoys reminding Juliet of this side of love and marriage:

> *"Go, girl, seek happy nights to happy days."*

and:

> *"I am the drudge and toil in your delight,"*

The nurse does not understand Juliet's love for Romeo and advises her to pretend to marry Paris in *Act 3 Scene V*:

> *"I think it best you married with the county.*
> *O! he's a lovely gentleman;*
> *Romeo's a dishclout to him:"*

Both Mercutio and Benvolio look on love in a more realistic way than Romeo. Benvolio, in *Act 1 Scene II*, advises Romeo to have more common sense in his attitude to love:

> *"Take thou some new infection to thy eye,*
> *And the rank poison of the old will die."*

Mercutio too sees Romeo's love for Rosaline as unrealistic and silly:

> *"If love be blind, love cannot hit the mark."*

While Mercutio is sensible, he sees love in terms of lust and physical pleasure:

> *"...this drivelling love is like a great natural,*
> *that runs lolling up and down to hide his bauble*
> *in a hole."*

and:

> *"If love be rough with you, be rough with love;*
> *Prick love for pricking, and you beat love down."*

However, he over-emphasises the physical side to balance Romeo's far-fetched notions of love.

(b) The Social and Moral Views of Love

Lady Capulet sees love in worldly terms. For her, love has little to do with romance and much to do with social advancement and status. She is, at thirty, much younger than her husband and did not marry for love. Her praise of Paris is extravagant:

> *"The valiant Paris seeks you for his love."*

She is conscious of how good a match with Paris, kinsman of the Prince, would be:

> *"So shall you share all that he doth possess,*
> *By having him, making yourself no less."*

Old Capulet, her husband, sees love as a father's duty. While he had promised to allow Juliet to choose her husband, he arranges a marriage to Paris without consulting her. This he sees as a father's duty to his daughter. Romance is unimportant to him.

> *ris, I will make a desperate tender*
> *child's love: I think she will be rul'd*
> *...ll respects by me; nay, more, I doubt it not."*

Paris seems to accept his view of love and marriage in *Act 4 Scene I:*

> *"My father Capulet will have it so;*
> *And I am nothing slow to slack his haste."*

Perhaps Paris believes that love will come to him and Juliet in time, but he is prepared to abide by an arranged marriage in *Act 4 Scene I.*

Friar Laurence accepts love as part of normal life, but records it as a young man's weakness:

> *"...young men's love then lies*
> *Not truly in their hearts, but in their eyes."*

Friar Laurence believes that love is sanctified by religion:

> *"So smile the heaven upon this holy act,"*

However, love must not be extreme; it must be tempered by restraint:

> *"These violent delights have violent ends,*
> *And in their triumph die, like fire and powder,*
> *Which, as they kiss consume..."*

> *"Therefore love moderately; long love doth so;*
> *Too swift arrives as tardy as too slow."*

(c) Romantic Love (Physical, Spiritual and Idealistic)

The love of Romeo and Juliet contrasts with the other ideas of love in the play since it is so pure and absolute and romantic. Yet their love embodies some of the physical, social and religious aspects of the other views of love in the play. It is these other views of love which help us to understand more fully the nature and extent of Romeo and Juliet's love, since they fall in love in a world with different and complicated views of love.

In *Act 1 Scene I* Romeo's love for Rosaline is impractical and defiant:

> *"Love is a smoke made with the fume of sighs;*
> *Being purg'd, a fire sparkling in lovers' eyes;*
> *Being vex'd, a sea nourished with lovers' tears:*
> *What is it else? a madness most discreet,*
> *A choking gall, and a preserving sweet."*

Romeo's love is not real love for another person and he is really *"in love with love"*, and Mercutio teases him for his silliness later on:

> *"If love be blind, love cannot hit the mark."*

Romeo, however, sees his love as:

> "...the devout religion of mine eye..."

But very soon he abandons this "religion":

> "I have forgot that name, and that name's woe."

Juliet's early attitude to love, before she meets Romeo, is one of innocence and modesty. She says in *Act 1 Scene III*:

> "It is an honour that I dream not of."

She would welcome love but does not expect to find it with Paris:

> "I'll look to like, if looking liking move;
> But no more deep will I endart mine eye
> Than your consent gives strength to make it fly."

It seems here that she will be guided in love by her parents' wishes. When Romeo and Juliet fall in love at Capulet's feast, the love of each is just as strong and absolute as the other's, but the effects of their passion on each other differ. In *Act 2 Scene II*, Juliet is deeply in love with Romeo but she is stronger and more practical than Romeo who answers her practical questions in imaginative and poetic terms.

> Juliet: "Art thou not Romeo, and a Montague?"
>
> Romeo: "Neither, fair maid, if either thee dislike."
>
> Juliet: "How cam'st thou hither, tell me, and wherefore?"
>
> Romeo: "With love's light wings did I o'erperch these walls;
>   ...And what love can do that dares love attempt;"

Thus romantic love differs from person to person but is no less real because of that.

The love of Romeo and Juliet is real and practical. Both Romeo and Juliet eagerly look forward to the happiness of their wedding night. Juliet says in *Act 3 Scene II* as she eagerly awaits her husband:

> "Come, gentle night; come, loving, black-brow'd night,
> Give me my Romeo:"

She is grief-stricken when she hears that Romeo killed Tybalt and is banished:

> "O break, my heart! — poor bankrupt, break at once!
> To prison, eyes, ne'er look on liberty!"

In *Act 3 Scene III*, Romeo's grief and despair are real but he is cheered up by the prospect of spending the night with Juliet:

> "But that a joy past joy calls out on me,
> It were a grief so brief to part from thee:"

In *Act 3 Scene V* we see that they have spent a night of absolute love and are loath to part from each other:

"Wilt thou be gone? It is not yet near day:"

When the lovers meet what seem to be insurmountable obstacles to their future together, their love becomes selfless and heroic. In *Act 4 Scene III* Juliet faces a marriage to Paris a day earlier than planned. Isolated from her husband and alienated from her family, she defies death itself by taking the friar's mysterious potion. Despite the horrors of the Capulet vault where she will be laid alive, she dedicates her sacrifice of self to Romeo:

"Romeo, I come! this do I drink to thee."

In *Act 5 Scene I* Romeo prepares to die to be with Juliet. His love too is heroic:

"Well, Juliet, I will lie with thee to-night."

In *Act 5 Scene III* Romeo dies with the words:

"Thus with a kiss I die."

and Juliet's last words are:

"O happy dagger!
This is thy sheath; there rust, and let me die."

Thus true love is spiritual as well as physical and can overcome misfortune and death in a heroic manner. True love brought maturity, courage and determination to the lovers as they overcame the obstacles to the fulfilment of their love. True love helped to reform society by reconciling the lovers' families. Thus the love of Romeo and Juliet is physical, practical, spiritual and idealistic as well as social and personal in its nature and effects.

D. Feud, Fate and Flaw

Both the feud (or civil disorder) on the streets of Verona and Fate (chance, accident, bad luck) play significant parts in *Romeo and Juliet*. It is debatable which contributes most to the tragedy. Whether a flaw in the hero's or heroine's character causes or contributes to the tragedy is also debatable.

In *Act 1 Scene I,* the feud is dramatised in a street battle involving servants and family members alike. In *Act 3 Scene I,* there is an atmosphere of hostility in the air and Benvolio tries to keep Mercutio off the streets to prevent a quarrel with Tybalt or his kinsmen. However, in *Act 1 Scene V,* Capulet is willing to overlook Romeo's presence at the feast and it seems that the feud is at a low ebb. However inactive the feud may be, it still does influence the secretive and hasty actions of the lovers in dealing with the problem of

Romeo's banishment, which was itself a direct result of the feud. Thus the feud is at least partly responsible for the misfortunes and deaths which befall the lovers.

Fate in the play takes the form of (a) frequent forebodings and references to fortune; (b) accidents or coincidences (such as Friar Laurence's delayed letter to Romeo or Romeo's early arrival at Juliet's tomb); and (c) the swift movement forward of the action of the play, leaving little time for either the characters or the audience to realise fully the significance of what is happening. There can be little doubt that the lovers experience bad luck (or fate) frequently in the play and thus Fate as well as the feud contribute together to Romeo's and Juliet's misfortunes and deaths.

It is true to say that Romeo is young and impractical. He is inclined to extremes of feeling and acts hastily. Juliet too is hasty in adopting the friar's desperate plan to save her from an embarrassing marriage to Paris. However, it would be far from true to say that any of these faults or all of them are the main cause of the tragedy.

Thus, while feud, Fate and flaws in character each contribute to the tragedy of the play, it is the combination of the three together which leads inevitably to the catastrophe. Indeed the tragedy is all the more intense since no single cause makes catastrophe inevitable. A spark in a fume-filled room can have devastating consequences without good luck!

In *Act 3 Scene I* the combination of these factors causes the crisis. We are reminded of the feud by Benvolio's advice to Mercutio to stay off the streets and by Tybalt's hot-blooded challenge to Romeo. Fate plays its part too since we already know of Tybalt's intention to challenge Romeo, but Romeo doesn't since he has not been at home the previous night. Romeo innocently and unknowingly tries to intervene between Tybalt and Mercutio, thus causing Mercutio's death. Thus the feud, Fate and Romeo's lack of knowledge of the true state of affairs co-operate to cause Romeo to slay Tybalt and incur banishment. Had Romeo been fully aware of how things stood, perhaps he might not have been caught up in the crisis of the play.

Development of Character

ROMEO

Romeo at the Beginning

In *Act 1 Scene I*, Romeo is the typical adolescent lover who is in love with an unattainable love, Rosaline. He is melancholy and seeks attention for his sadness. He is ready for love but has not yet found it:

> *"Many a morning hath he there been seen,*
> *With tears augmenting the fresh morning's dew,*
> *Adding to clouds more clouds with his deep sighs;"*

This is his father's estimate of him.

Romeo Meets Juliet

When Romeo meets Juliet in *Act 1 Scene V*, he abandons his former adolescent love and falls deeply and passionately in love with Juliet, calling her *"This holy shrine"*. He is transformed from a reluctant lover to an eager one. From then on, he defies danger and the Capulets by entering Capulet's orchard to see Juliet. His mind is purified and his love is sincere and strong:

> *"Call me but love, and I'll be new baptiz'd;*
> *Henceforth I never will be Romeo."*

He is still lost in a world of imagination as Juliet makes the arrangements for their marriage:

> *"How silver-sweet sound lovers' tongues by night,*
> *Like softest music to attending ears!"*

When Romeo meets his friends in *Act 2 Scene IV,* Mercutio notices how Romeo has changed and remarks:

> *"Why, is this not better now than groaning for love?*
> *now art thou sociable, now art thou Romeo;"*

But Romeo still has not come down to earth.

Romeo Married

After his marriage to Juliet, Romeo is a new man, with a sense of responsibility and honour. In *Act 3 Scene I* he tries to treat Tybalt as a kinsman whom he loves. When Tybalt slays Romeo's friend, Mercutio, Romeo avenges Mercutio's death as a debt of honour:

> *"...O sweet Juliet!*
> *Thy beauty hath made me effeminate,*
> *And in my temper soften'd valour's steel!"*

In the friar's cell later *(Act 3 Scene III)* Romeo loses his nerve temporarily but becomes a man again when he hears from Juliet, through the nurse, that she needs him to comfort her. In the second balcony scene *(Act 3 Scene V)*, it is Romeo who is more practical and sensible than Juliet:

> *"I must be gone and live, or stay and die."*

He is also tender and loving:

> "Farewell!
> I will omit no opportunity
> That may convey my greetings, love, to thee."

Romeo in Exile

Romeo, in exile in *Act 5 Scene I,* seems in happy mood, looking forward to news from the friar that he may return to Juliet. Suddenly he hears of Juliet's "death", but does not despair or falter in self-control. Calmly he reacts to the news:

> "Is it even so? then I defy you, stars!"

He plans to be united with Juliet in death and buys poison. At the vault in *Act 5 Scene III,* Romeo is decisive and allows no obstacle to stand in the way of his tragic purpose. He kills Paris but lays him by Juliet's side in atonement. He heroically sacrifices himself for love by taking poison, saying: *"Thus with a kiss I die."* Thus has true love transformed Romeo from a moody youth to a more mature and heroic adult. Yet Romeo has still not fully understood the destructiveness of his absolute love, which, in the thoughtless world of Verona, can only be fulfilled in his own death.

JULIET

Juliet at the Beginning

In *Act 1 Scene III,* Juliet is an innocent and dutiful daughter to the Capulets. She is not yet fourteen, the nurse informs us. Juliet intends to co-operate with her parents wishes that she marry Paris:

> "I'll look to like, if looking liking move."

However, she does not promise to marry Paris but she will try to love him for her parents' sake.

Juliet meets Romeo

When Juliet meets Romeo in *Act 1 Scene V,* she falls in love for the first time and reacts affectionately and sincerely to Romeo's attempts to woo her. In the Balcony Scene, *Act 2 Scene II,* she expresses her deep love for Romeo:

> "My bounty is as boundless as the sea,
> My love as deep; the more I give to thee,
> The more I have, for both are infinite."

She is practical and warns Romeo of the danger to his life if he is caught with her. It is she who suggests the arrangements for their marriage. In *Act 2 Scene V,* we see the longing and impatience of Juliet to be with her lover. In the marriage scene, Juliet declares her absolute love for Romeo:

> *"But my true love is grown to such excess*
> *I cannot sum up sum of half my wealth."*

Juliet under Stress

Just after the lovers' sad farewell, Juliet is confronted with an arranged marriage to Paris, which she rejects decisively:

> *"Now, by Saint Peter's church, and Peter too,*
> *He shall not make me there a joyful bride."*

In her subsequent alienation from her parents and the nurse, Juliet shows strength and endurance.

> *"I'll to the friar, to know his remedy:*
> *If all else fail, myself have power to die."*

In *Act 4 Scene III*, Juliet shows heroic courage as, all alone, she takes the friar's potion a day earlier than intended. Despite the horrors she imagines of being buried alive in the Capulet vault, she does not hesitate to abandon herself completely to her love for Romeo:

> *"Romeo, I come! this do I drink to thee."*

Juliet in the Vault

When Juliet awakens in the vault, she finds Romeo dead. She does not despair but firmly refuses to leave the tomb with the friar. She shows heroic courage and resolution in killing herself with Romeo's dagger. In a sense she has already overcome death in *Act 4 Scene III* by taking the potion, but she "dies" again with love on her lips:

> *"O happy dagger!*
> *"This is thy sheath; there rust, and let me die."*

Thus Juliet too was transformed by love from an innocent child to a woman of heroic strength and self-sacrifice. She seems to have a better understanding of love and how ill-fated absolute love is in a society which is thoughtless and even antagonistic. Yet she comes closer to the reality of her situation than Romeo does and she is perhaps the real tragic heroine of the play.

MERCUTIO

While Mercutio is portrayed as a real personality in the play, his character does not have time to change or develop since he dies in *Act 3 Scene I*. Mercutio is light-hearted and witty and his gaiety contrasts with Romeo's melancholy in *Act 1 Scene IV*. He teases Romeo about his infatuation for Rosaline:

> *"You are a lover; borrow Cupid's wings;*
> *And soar with them above a common bound."*

Mercutio is more realistic than Romeo and sees that real love must be grounded in the reality of the world around him. In *Act 1 Scene IV* he tries to advise Romeo to be more practical and to express his real feelings and desires:

> *"If love be rough with you, be rough with love;*
> *Prick love for pricking, and you beat love down."*

Romeo is unable to accept this realism *(Act 2, Scene II)*:

> *"He jests at scars, that never felt a wound."*

Mercutio is a loyal friend whose qualities equal if not surpass Romeo's.

Mercutio is also cynical at times and denounces pretence or sham. He is disgusted when Romeo misreads Tybalt's challenge in *Act 3 Scene I* and refuses to fight:

> *"O calm, dishonourable, vile submission!"*

Mercutio loves wordplay and swordplay and sneers at Tybalt's swordsmanship:

> *"Will you pluck your sword out of his*
> *pilcher by the ears?"*

Unlike Tybalt, Mercutio bears no malice and dies cursing both houses:

> *"A plague o' both your houses!"*

He is neutral in the feud and fights Tybalt to preserve Romeo's honour and his own safety. But for Romeo's interference, his skill as a swordsman would have defeated Tybalt and the feud would have been lessened, at least temporarily. In a sense, then, he is a peacemaker, whose untimely death prevented his efforts at restoring peace from being effective. However, he is most memorable in the play for his intelligent and imaginitive, if bawdy, humour, which relieves tension.

THE NURSE

The nurse's character in the play does not undergo any development, but she is important as Juliet's messenger and adviser and she lends realism to the romance of the play.

She is worldly and practical and has no scruples about Juliet marrying Paris immorally:

> *"I think it best you married with the county.*
> *O! he's a lovely gentleman;"*

She had already praised Romeo, but has changed her mind as circumstances changed. She contrasts with Juliet's fidelity to love of Romeo.

She is vulgar and enjoys reminding Juliet of the physical side of love:

> *"Go, girl, seek happy nights to happy days."*

She is garrulous and enjoys teasing or interrupting others. In *Act 2 Scene V,* when Juliet is anxious for news of her marriage plans, the nurse delays telling her, complaining of weariness.

> *"Fie, how my bones ache!"*

Despite her shortcomings, the nurse is loyal to Juliet throughout the play. She meets Romeo to arrange the marriage, she provides a ladder so that the lovers may be together and she fetches Romeo from Friar Laurence's when Juliet needs him to comfort her. She says to Romeo:

> *'For Juliet's sake, for her sake, rise and stand;"*

Yet Juliet dismisses her from her confidence since the nurse cannot give her the understanding she needs:

> *"Thou and my bosom henceforth shall be twain."*

The nurse's realism and worldliness highlight the depth of Juliet's idealism and love.

FRIAR LAURENCE

Friar Laurence's role in the play is very important. He is Romeo's adviser and friend. He performs the wedding ceremony of Romeo and Juliet. He provides the potion for Juliet to avoid a marriage to Paris. He undertakes to persuade the hostile families to accept the lovers' marriage in *Act 3 Scene III,* but has little time to do so before catastrophe takes place. He wishes to bring peace to Verona but fails. His intentions are good, but his plans go tragically wrong.

As a person he is a holy and deep-thinking old man who has a good reputation in the city for holiness and charitable works. He is well versed in the medicinal uses of herbs and tries to use his knowledge for the good of others. His advice to Romeo is appropriate:

> *"Therefore love moderately; long love doth so;*
> *Too swift arrives as tardy as too slow."*

Despite his good advice, Friar Laurence is too hasty himself in forming his ill-conceived and risky plan to put Juliet to sleep. However, it is his kindness of heart that makes him take the risk, since Juliet can find no other solution:

> *"Hold, daughter; I do spy a kind of hope,*
> *Which craves as desperate an execution*
> *As that is desperate which we would prevent."*

In the end Friar Laurence becomes demoralised by the failure of his plan and loses his composure, leaving Juliet to kill herself in the vault. He must bear moral responsibility for the deaths of Romeo and Juliet.

THE PARENTS

The Montague and Capulet parents are not finely drawn characters in the play. However, they each exhibit some traits of character which are important in the development of the play.

In the first scene Capulet is more comical than serious as he attempts to fight and his wife advises he needs a crutch instead. Later in the scene, Montague shows real concern for the welfare of his son, Romeo. Lady Montague too seems to love her son and dies of grief at his banishment. Both Montague and Capulet are generous to each other's children in *Act 5 Scene III* when they outdo each other in the monuments they propose to erect for each other's children. They genuinely desire a new beginning and have learned their lessons.

Capulet and his wife are revealed a little more than the Montagues as the play proceeds. Lady Capulet is about thirty years old and seems to have married Capulet for social advancement. She is very anxious for Juliet to marry Paris because of the status:

> *"So shall you share all that he doth possess,*
> *By having him, making yourself no less."*

However, she is cold and unfeeling in her dismissal of Juliet in *Act 3 Scene V*:

> *"Do as thou wilt, for I have done with thee."*

It is she too who seeks revenge for Tybalt's death:

> *"Romeo slew Tybalt, Romeo must not live."*

Capulet, in *Act 1 Scene II*, seems to be a considerate father who will allow his daughter to choose her husband. However, in *Act 3 Scene IV*, he promises her in marriage to Paris without consulting her, saying:

> *"I think she will be rul'd*
> *In all respects by me;"*

In *Act 3 Scene V* he shows a cruel lack of understanding and coldly disowns his only daughter:

> *"...beg, starve, die in the streets,*
> *For, by my soul, I'll ne'er acknowledge thee,"*

However, his attitude was typical of the society of the time and he was motivated more by duty than by cruelty. Another point in his favour was his acceptance of Romeo at the feast, showing his hospitable nature, which is also displayed in his lavish preparations for Paris's wedding to Juliet.

TYBALT

Tybalt is almost a caricature and not a real character. His one role is to display hot temper and anger which provoke the crisis in *Act 3 Scene I*.

At the Capulet feast he recognises Romeo as a Montague and desires to fight. Later, in *Act 3 Scene I*, we see that Tybalt still holds a grudge against Romeo for the previous incident:

> *"Romeo, the love I bear thee can afford*
> *No better term than this, — thou art a villain."*

Mercutio despises Tybalt for his showy swordplay and perhaps his sham bravery (Romeo is able to defeat Tybalt with little difficulty).

Tybalt's main purpose in the play is to embody the spirit of hostility and revenge which is widespread among the Capulets and the Montagues. Perhaps it is the feud that created characters such as Tybalt, who may not be the real villain.

BENVOLIO

Benvolio's main role in the play is that of peacemaker, who repeatedly intervenes on the side of peace and common sense in the play.

In the first scene, Benvolio tries to stop the brawl between the servants. He later *(Act 3 Scene I)* tries to keep Mercutio off the streets since *"the Capulets are abroad"*. He intervenes on the side of Romeo when the Prince is trying to sort out the blame. His version of what happened is unbiased and entirely truthful, apportioning the blame on Tybalt mainly but also on Romeo.

Benvolio's other role is that of comforter and friend to Romeo. Benvolio tries to help Romeo to overcome his melancholy and gives him sound advice. Romeo should examine other solutions to his emotional state by getting to know other women:

> *"By giving liberty unto thine eyes:*
> *Examine other beauties."*

Benvolio sees an opportunity for a solution in going to Capulet's feast where Romeo will meet other women:

> *"...some other maid*
> *That I will show you shining at this feast,*
> *And she shall scant show well that now shows best."*

PRINCE ESCALUS

The Prince is a symbol of order and authority in the play rather than a person. He is highly respected by all in his meting out of justice. He threatens death to anyone who causes further trouble after the street brawl in *Act 1 Scene I*:

> *"If ever you disturb our streets again*
> *Your lives shall pay the forfeit of the peace."*

However, he tempers justice with mercy and banishes Romeo instead of carrying out his threat of death, since Romeo was not totally to blame for Tybalt's death.

In the end he shows the hostile families how they are responsible for the deaths of Romeo and Juliet and he is instrumental in bringing about the reconciliation of the families.

> *"See what a scourge is laid upon your hate,*
> *That heaven finds means to kill your joys with love;"*

He is fair and merciful and represents peace and justice in the play.

> *"Thy fault our law calls death; but the kind prince,*
> *Taking thy part, hath rush'd aside the law,*
> *And turn'd that black word death to banishment:*
> *This is dear mercy, and thou seest it not."*

is Friar Laurence's estimate of the Prince in *Act 3 Scene III*.

PARIS

Paris is unusual in that he is not an old, unattractive suitor for Juliet, but is young, handsome and a kinsman of the Prince. He shows consideration for Juliet when he suggests to Friar Laurence that marriage will be good for Juliet, since she is grieving too much for Tybalt's death. He agrees to marry her in obedience to her father's proposal. He seems to regard the marriage as desireable since Juliet is beautiful and from a noble family.

There is evidence to suggest that in *Act 5 Scene III* Paris goes to Juliet's tomb to perform a farewell ceremony. Perhaps he had begun to love Juliet since his last meeting with her in Friar Laurence's cell since he calls his ceremony *"true love's rite"*. He is courageous in defending the tomb from desecration by Romeo and his last wish is to lie with Juliet in death:

> *"...If thou be merciful,*
> *Open the tomb, lay me with Juliet."*

Even though his intended marriage to Juliet hastened her death, Paris is not to blame, since he had no knowledge of the true state of affairs. Paris is not the villain of the play, but his main role is to provide a contrast to Romeo's passion and intensity. He is cool and polite in his attitude to Juliet, whereas Romeo is hot and passionate in his love.

Questions

Act 1

Scene I

1. Outline the background information provided in this scene on Verona, the setting of the play.
2. Does Romeo gain your sympathy in this scene? Give reasons.
3. What is the purpose of the street brawl in this scene?

Scene II

1. Describe Capulet's attitude to his daughter in this scene. Do you agree with him? Give reasons.
2. How would you rate Paris as a suitor for Juliet? Give reasons.
3. Describe Romeo's mood in this scene. What is his real problem?

Scene III

1. Do you find the nurse annoying or amusing in this scene? Give reasons.
2. Describe Lady Capulet's attitude to Juliet in this scene. Do you regard her as a good mother? Give reasons.
3. Is Juliet too young to marry? Give reasons.

Scene IV

1. Do you agree with Mercutio's attitude to love? Give reasons.
2. What do you find amusing or entertaining about Mercutio? Give examples.
3. Is Romeo's sadness real or imaginary? Give reasons.

Scene V

1. Why is Old Capulet taking Romeo's side in this scene? Give reasons.
2. Describe how and why Romeo and Juliet fall in love.
3. Do you think Tybalt is justified in his attitude to Romeo? Give reasons.
4. Why is this scene of great significance in the play?

Act 2

Scene I

1. Describe Mercutio's and Benvolio's attitudes to Romeo and his love.
2. Why does Romeo try to escape from his companions?

Scene II

1. Describe the atmosphere of this scene.
2. Compare and contrast Romeo's and Juliet's attitudes to love and to each other.
3. How have Romeo and Juliet changed since *Act 1 Scene V*?

Scene III

1. Is Friar Laurence a good friend to Romeo? Give reasons.
2. Why does the friar agree to Romeo's marriage plans? Is he right?
3. How does the friar's character differ from Romeo's?

Scene IV

1. Why are Romeo's friends worried for his safety in this scene? Are they justified?
2. How has Romeo changed in this scene?
3. Why is this scene amusing? Give examples.
4. How does this scene advance the action of the play?

Scene V

1. Describe the different moods of Juliet in this scene.
2. Do you sympathise with the nurse's tiredness in this scene? Why?
3. Has Juliet changed much since the Balcony Scene?

Scene VI

1. Is Romeo really in love this time? Give reasons.
2. Which of the two, Romeo or Juliet, do you think is most in love?
3. Describe the friar's attitude to the lovers in this scene.

Act 3

Scene I

1. Why is this scene the crisis scene?
2. What changes take place in Romeo's character in this scene? Are they changes for the better? Give reasons.
3. Who or what is most to blame for the deaths in this scene? Give reasons.
4. This is a scene of contrasting characters and attitudes. Explain with examples.
5. Is it fair that Romeo should be banished? Give reasons.
6. What might have happened, had Romeo not interfered?

Scene II

1. Describe Juliet's mood at the beginning of this scene.
2. Has Juliet's attitude to Romeo changed by the end of the scene? Give reasons.
3. This scene is a crisis for Juliet. How well does she cope with it?

Scene III

1. Does Romeo let down Juliet in this scene?
2. How does the friar plan to help Romeo? Is he realistic?
3. What helps Romeo to recover from despair in this scene?

Scene IV

1. Is Capulet a concerned father or a cruel tyrant in this scene? Give reasons.
2. Is Paris worthy to marry Juliet?
3. Does Capulet understand his daughter?

Scene V

1. How are Romeo's and Juliet's roles reversed in this scene?
2. Is Lady Capulet really trying to help Juliet in this scene? Give reasons.
3. Is Juliet expecting too much from the nurse in this scene? Give reasons.
4. Juliet isolates herself, in this scene, from her parents and the nurse. Is she justified? Could she have found an easier solution?

Act 4

Scene I

1. How does Paris compare with Romeo as a suitable husband for Juliet?
2. What is the friar's plan to help the lovers? Do its disadvantages outweigh its advantages? What alternatives has he?
3. Is Juliet strong or weak in this scene? Give reasons.

Scene II

1. Is Juliet deceitful in this scene? Give reasons.
2. Is Old Capulet childish in this scene? Give reasons.

Scene III

1. Is Juliet too hasty in taking the friar's potion? Give reasons.
2. Is Juliet right to take the potion, which she realises may kill her?
3. Does Juliet take the potion for love or to escape an immoral marriage to Paris?

Scene IV

1. What is Capulet trying to prove by his elaborate preparations for the wedding feast?
2. What is the purpose of this scene? Is it to relieve or create tension?

Scene V

1. Is the grief of this scene real? Give reasons.
2. Describe the friar's attitude in this scene.
3. Would it be better if Juliet were really dead in this scene? Give reasons.

Act 5
Scene I

1. How well has Romeo coped with his banishment?
2. How is Romeo more admirable in this scene than ever before?
3. What are Romeo's plans? Is he right?

Scene II

1. Was Friar Laurence careless or slow? Give reasons.
2. Is this scene significant in the play as a whole? Give reasons.

Scene III

1. Describe the atmosphere of this scene.
2. Do you sympathise with Paris in this scene? Is he too hasty or rash?
3. Compare Juliet's suicide to Romeo's.
4. Is Friar Laurence really a coward in this scene?
5. Does this scene end sadly or happily? Give reasons.

Examination Questions
JUNIOR CERTIFICATE ENGLISH: HIGHER LEVEL

2004
Section 1: Drama

Question Two: Answer **EITHER 1 OR 2.**

1. Name a play you have studied in which one character rebels against another. With
   which character did you have more sympathy? Give reasons for your answer making
   reference to the play.   (30)

OR

2. Name a play you have studied.

Choose a scene from this play you found either happy **or** sad.

Describe how the playwright conveys this happiness **or** sadness.   (30)

2005

Section 1: Drama

Question Two: Answer **EITHER 1 OR 2.**

1. Select a play you have studied and choose from it a scene where conflict occurs.

(a) Outline what happens in this scene.   (10)

(b) What are the underlying causes of the conflict in this scene?

Support your answer by reference to the play as a whole.   (20)

OR

2. Choose your favourite character from a play you have studied.

(a) Why do you find this character interesting? Support your answer by reference to the text.   (10)

(b) Discuss the relationship between your chosen character and **ONE** other character in the play. Refer to the text in support of your answer.   (20)

2006

Section 1: Drama

Question Two: Answer **EITHER 1 OR 2.**

1. Consider a character from a play you have studied. Choose a significant time of *either* good luck *or* bad luck which this character experiences.

(a) Briefly describe this experience of good luck *or* bad luck.   (15)

(b) Discuss how the character deals with it in the play.   (15)

OR

2. 'Plays teach us lessons about life.'

Choose any play you have studied and explain how it has made you aware of any one of the following:

Love *or* Death *or* Conflict *or* Harmony.

Explain your answer by reference to your chosen play.   (30)

2007

Section 1: Drama

Question Two: Answer **EITHER 1 OR 2.**

1. Name a play you have studied and state what you think is its main idea and/or message. Explain how this main idea and/or message is communicated in the play. (30)

OR

2. You have been asked to recommend a play for students studying for the Junior Certificate. Would you recommend the play you have studied for this examination? Give reasons based on close reference to your chosen text.   (30)

2008

Section 1: Drama

Question Two: Answer **EITHER 1 OR 2.**

1. Many dramas feature characters that are either winners or losers. Choose a character from a play you have studied who falls into one of these categories.

   (a) Describe how your chosen character is either a winner or a loser.   (10)

   (b) Choose another character who has a relationship with your chosen character, and explain the importance of this relationship.

   Support your answer with reference to your studied text.   (20)

OR

2. Imagine you are preparing a programme for a class production of a play you have studied. The production team, of which you are a part, has asked you to contribute to the programme.

   (a) Write character profiles for two characters who have a significant role in the play.   (15)

   (b) Write an introduction to the play focusing especially on its theme(s).   (15)

   To keep the programme to an appropriate length you will need to write approximately 200 words for task (a) and approximately 200 words for task (b).

JUNIOR CERTIFICATE ENGLISH: ORDINARY LEVEL

2004

Section 6: Drama

Question E

   Name a **PLAY** or a **FILM** you have studied.

   Using **ONE** of the following headings, write about the play or film.

   – The scene I liked best.

   – The character I found most interesting.

   – Why I found the play/film enjoyable.

   – Why I did not enjoy the play/film.   (20)

2005

Section 6: Drama

Question E

Name a **PLAY** or a **FILM** you have studied.

Pick the scene you remember best from the play or the film and write about:

- what exactly happened
- how any **ONE** character behaved
- what especially makes you remember the scene you have chosen.   (20)

2006

Section 6: Drama

Question E

Name a **PLAY** or **FILM** you have studied in which a disagreement occurs.

- What caused the disagreement?
- Was the disagreement settled? Why? Why not?
- Were you satisfied with the ending? Give reasons for your answer.   (20)

2007

Section 6: Drama

Question E

1. Name a play or film you have studied in which something very unexpected happens. Describe the unexpected event and explain why it was unexpected.   (10)
2. Did the unexpected event add to your enjoyment of the studied play or film? Explain why/why not?   (10)

2008

Section 6: Drama

Question E

Name a **PLAY** or **FILM** you have studied in which a character has an important dream or ambition which he/she succeeds or fails in making real.

- What was the dream or ambition?
- How did it succeed or fail?
- What effect did this success or failure have on the character in question?
- Would you recommend this film or play to your friends? Why/Why not?   (20)